Discover & Learn

Locations

Teacher Book

This Teacher Book accompanies CGP's Discover & Learn Locations Geography books for Key Stage Two.

It includes background information to help teachers introduce and teach each topic, answers to Activity Book questions and varied suggestions for extra activities.

It's the perfect guide to planning and delivering Locations Geography lessons throughout KS2!

Contents

Published by CGP

Consultant: Joanna Copley

Contributors: Mai Black, Catherine Hitchcock, Amanda MacNaughton

Editors: Mary Falkner, Sarah Pattison, Rosa Roberts, Rebecca Russell, Caroline Thomson

With thanks to Felicity Booth, Harriet Foster, Glenn Rogers and Rachael Rogers for the proofreading.
With thanks to Jan Greenway for the copyright research.

National Curriculum references throughout reproduced under the terms of the Open Government Licence v3.0.
http://www.nationalarchives.gov.uk/doc/open-government-licence/version/3/

Page 25 renewable data from IRENA (2018), Renewable Energy Statistics 2018, The International Renewable Energy Agency, Abu Dhabi.

CIA World Fact Book - energy data on p45 from The World Factbook: Washington DC, Central Intelligence Agency, 2019

When using the Extra Activities in this product, please take the safety of the participants into consideration at all times, and ensure that children are supervised when researching material for this product online. Teachers should also take into account pupils' personal circumstances when dealing with topics of a sensitive nature.

ISBN: 978 1 78294 988 6

Printed by Elanders Ltd, Newcastle upon Tyne

Meet the UK

Study Book (pages 2-3)

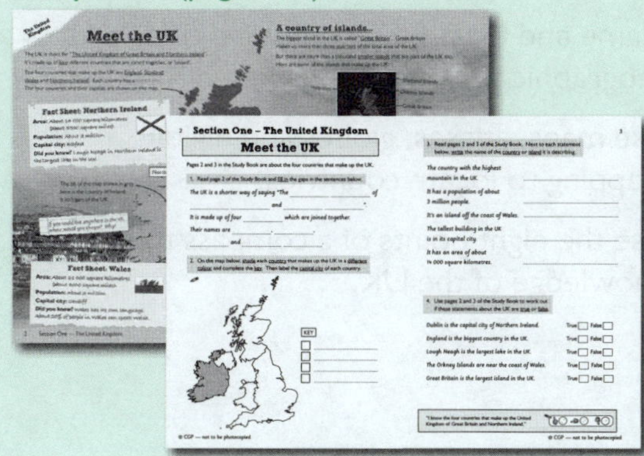

Activity Book (pages 2-3)

National Curriculum Aims

- Name and locate the countries, cities and geographic regions of the United Kingdom.

- Use maps, atlases, globes and digital mapping to locate countries.

Introduction

The UK is made up of four countries, which were once independent nations. Wales was ruled by England from the end of the 13th century, and became part of the Kingdom of England under the Acts of Union in 1536 and 1543. The United Kingdom of Great Britain was created in 1707 with the union of the Kingdom of Scotland and the Kingdom of England. Ireland joined the union in 1801, but most of Ireland left the union in 1922 after the Irish War of Independence. Six counties in the north of Ireland remained in the union, becoming Northern Ireland. So the new country became the United Kingdom of Great Britain and Northern Ireland.

Answers to Activity Book Questions

1. *The UK is a shorter way of saying "The* United Kingdom *of* Great Britain *and* Northern Ireland". *It is made up of four* countries *which are joined together. Their names are* England, Scotland, Wales *and* Northern Ireland.

2. Pupils should have correctly shaded in the countries of the UK, and the key should match the colours used on their map. Pupils should also have marked the capital cities in the appropriate locations.

3. Scotland, Wales, Anglesey, England, Northern Ireland

4. False — True — True — False — True

Extra Activities

- Use an interactive whiteboard and ask pupils to identify the UK on Google Earth™ mapping service, and explore the different regions and countries. Include a look at the pupils' own home town(s) and school. Provide pupils with blank maps of the UK so that they can mark on major cities and geographical features, such as mountain ranges and lakes. Some possible features include: Glasgow, Leeds, Birmingham, Bristol, Londonderry, Swansea, the Pennines, Snowdonia, the Grampian Mountains, the Mourne Mountains, Lough Neagh, Loch Ness, Loch Morar, Windermere. Pass a globe around the class so that each pupil has the chance to find the UK and relate its position to Europe and other continents.

- Get pupils to ask an adult at home about a friend or relative who lives in a different part of the UK. Alternatively, pupils could select a famous person who lives in the UK. Get pupils to pin a picture or the name of their chosen person to the relevant place on a map of the UK.

- Ask pupils to look at pages 2 and 3 of the Study Book (or an atlas) and give them two minutes to memorise the shape of the UK, the borders of the four countries and their capital cities. After that, pupils could be given a blank piece of paper and try to recreate the map from memory. At the end, pupils can compare their maps with the original and self-assess their work on a scale of one to five for: a) the shape of the coastline, b) the position of borders, c) the location of capital cities.

The Organisation of the UK

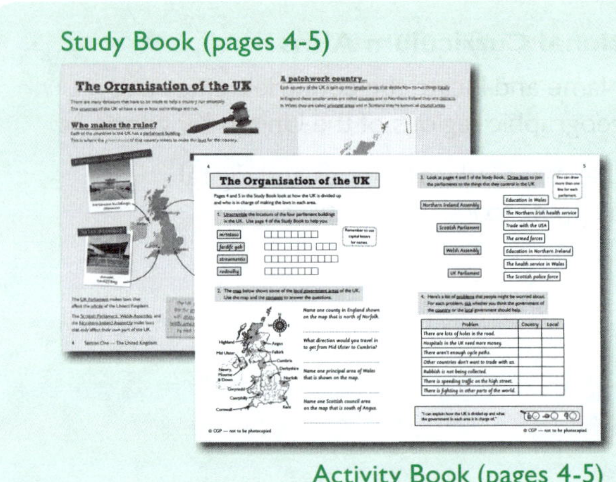

Activity Book (pages 4-5)

National Curriculum Aims

- Name and locate the countries, cities and geographic regions of the United Kingdom.

- Use maps, atlases, globes and digital mapping to locate countries.

- Use the eight points of a compass to build knowledge of the UK.

Introduction

The way that the UK is divided up has changed over time, as has the way in which it's governed. Counties, council areas, principal areas and districts are based on historic county divisions, with 48 counties in England, 32 council areas in Scotland, 22 principal areas in Wales and 11 districts in Northern Ireland. Some counties in England have been divided up further for local administration purposes. Acts of parliament that created devolved parliaments for Wales and Scotland were established in 1998 after referendums in 1997. The Northern Ireland assembly was also created in 1998, as part of the Good Friday Agreement.

This topic provides the opportunity to discuss with pupils the concept of British values, particularly democracy and the rule of law, as well as who is in charge of making the laws where they live.

Answers to Activity Book Questions

1. Stormont — Cardiff Bay — Westminster — Holyrood

2. Derbyshire/Cumbria — East — Gwynedd/Caerphilly — Falkirk

3. Northern Ireland Assembly — The Northern Irish health service, Education in Northern Ireland
   Scottish Parliament — The Scottish police force
   Welsh Assembly — Education in Wales, The health service in Wales
   UK Parliament — Trade with the USA, The armed forces

4. local — country — local — country — local — local — country

Extra Activities

- Divide the class into teams and give each team four cards with pictures showing the UK parliament buildings. Read out a series of statements, each about one of the parliament buildings, to the class — for each statement, ask the teams to hold up the card for the parliament they think it applies to. The statements could be related to location (e.g. it is the furthest north, it is in the capital city of the UK, etc.) or to the things they control.

- Invite a local representative to talk to pupils about what their job entails. This could be their local MP, the mayor or a town councillor. Pupils could be asked to prepare questions before the local representative's visit. Pupils could also make thank you cards afterwards saying what they have learnt and if they have ambitions to get involved in politics later in life.

- In pairs, or as a class, pupils can visit www.ordnancesurvey.co.uk/mapzone and go to the games section and click on 'puzzle adventure'. Pupils can complete puzzles of the different countries in the UK to help them learn the position of the different countries and their local government areas. Alternatively, pupils could stick paper maps onto card and then cut them up to make their own jigsaw puzzles for a partner to solve.

In the City

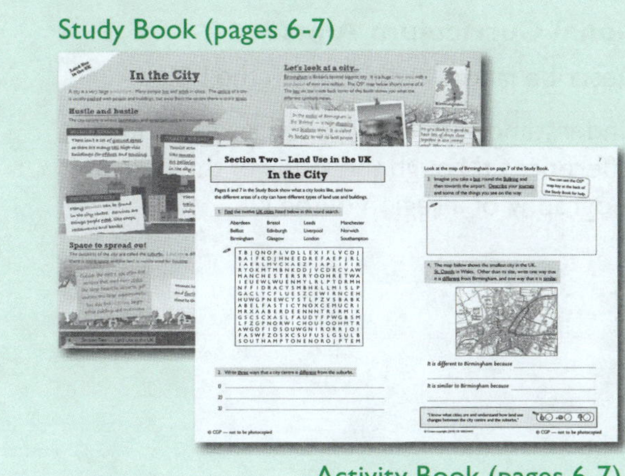

Study Book (pages 6-7)

Activity Book (pages 6-7)

National Curriculum Aims

- Describe land use patterns in the UK.

- Understand geographical similarities and differences through the study of the human geography of a region of the UK.

Introduction

This topic looks at land use in cities. Before studying this topic, pupils could be asked to discuss the types of land use that are present in the area that they live and in different places that they might have visited.

Answers to Activity Book Questions

1. On the right are the locations of the twelve cities in the grid:

2. Any three from: e.g. houses in suburbs are usually further apart/larger, buildings are taller in the city centre, there are more tourist attractions in the city centre, airports/hospitals/golf courses tend to be in the suburbs, a lot of services are in the city centre.

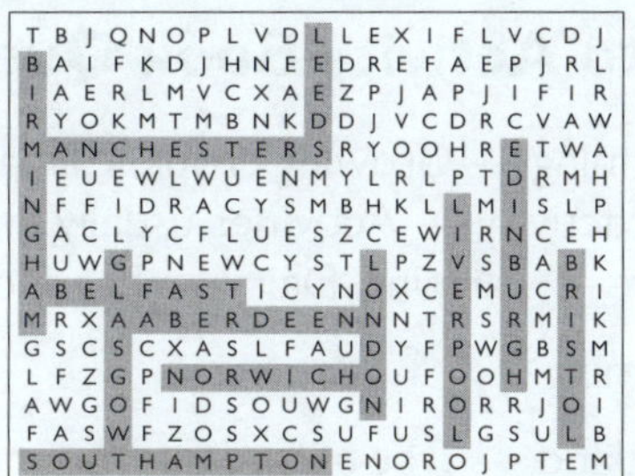

3. Any appropriate answer, including what might be seen in the city centre (e.g. shops, tall buildings, lots of people) and how it changes towards the airport (e.g. bigger houses, more space, fewer people).

4. Any appropriate answer. E.g. *It is different to Birmingham because* St Davids has fewer houses/main roads than Birmingham / St Davids doesn't have an airport/university. *It is similar to Birmingham because* buildings are closer together in the middle of the cities / main roads go into the city centre.

Extra Activities

- Ask pupils to compare the map of Birmingham on page 7 of the Study Book with a map of their local area. On a large piece of paper they should draw two overlapping circles using a plate to form a Venn diagram. On the right side they should write things that are only in Birmingham (e.g. the Bullring) and on the left side they should write things that are only in their local area (e.g. certain shops or museums). In the middle they should list things that are found in both places. If the pupils' local area is Birmingham, select a different city.

- In pairs or groups, get pupils to plan a weekend trip to Birmingham. Ask the pupils to use tourism leaflets or online resources to look for a place to stay and to decide which places and sights they would like to visit. They could then mark these locations on a map of the city. More advanced pupils could also write a structured itinerary for their stay.

- Give pupils a list of the population sizes of the UK's five biggest cities, as well as the total population size of the UK (approximately 66 000 000). In small groups, pupils could decide how to represent the information (e.g. pictogram, bar chart). After discussing as a class, pupils could then work individually to make their data display. More advanced pupils could be challenged to work out the fraction or percentage of the UK's total population that live in each of the five cities.

In the Country

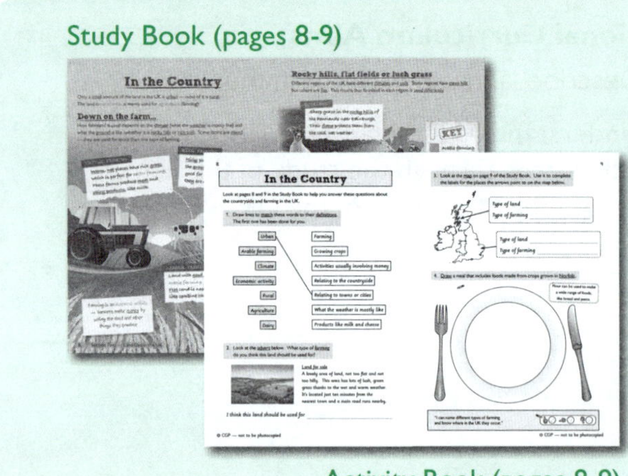

Study Book (pages 8-9)

Activity Book (pages 8-9)

National Curriculum Aims

- Describe land use patterns in the UK.
- Understand geographical similarities and differences through the study of the human geography of a region of the UK.

Introduction

Around 70% of land in the UK is used for agriculture and about 11% is used for urban or developed areas, but the majority of people live in urban areas. This topic provides pupils with the opportunity to think about how land is used in rural areas and where food comes from.

Answers to Activity Book Questions

1. Arable farming — Growing crops, Climate — What the weather is mostly like, Economic activity — Activities usually involving money, Rural — Relating to the countryside, Agriculture — Farming, Dairy — Products like milk and cheese

2. Cattle farming

3. West Scotland — *Type of land* e.g. mountainous. *Type of farming* hill (or sheep)
   Eastern England — *Type of land* e.g. flat. *Type of farming* arable

4. Any appropriate drawing, which could include wheat products (e.g. flour), carrots, potatoes and sugar.

Extra Activities

- Get pupils to imagine they are potato farmers. Split them into groups and give each group 50 tokens (such as plastic counters) to spend. Give them set prices for seed potatoes (1 token for five), fertiliser (4 tokens for fertiliser for 100 potato plants), workers (one worker needed per 100 plants, 10 tokens per worker) and farm buildings (each stores 1000 potatoes and costs 20 tokens). Pupils can decide how much to buy of each item and keep track of their spending. Each seed potato they plant will produce 10 potatoes, but if they use fertiliser it will produce 20. If they don't have enough workers or buildings, the extra potatoes will rot in the fields and they can't sell them. Pupils should decide how much to sell produce for (to the teacher, who can haggle over prices if they are not reasonable). Pupils can then calculate whether they have made a profit or a loss, and discuss how it could be improved in the future.

- Take pupils to visit a farm. They could prepare for the visit by looking at an aerial photograph and discussing how they think the land might be used. Pupils could prepare questions about the farm and the farmers' day-to-day life. During the visit, they could use a printed outline of the farm to note down how the different fields and buildings are being used.

- Ask pupils to compare and contrast two different farms: one local to them, and one in a non-European country, such as the rice paddy fields in Tamil Nadu, India. Look at both places on Google Earth™ mapping service. Split the class into groups. Each group can use the internet to gather information about one of the following: climate, seasonal changes, features of the land, crops and animals. Pupils could write up their findings with at least one graph or table to show information clearly.

Changes in Land Use

Study Book (pages 10-11)

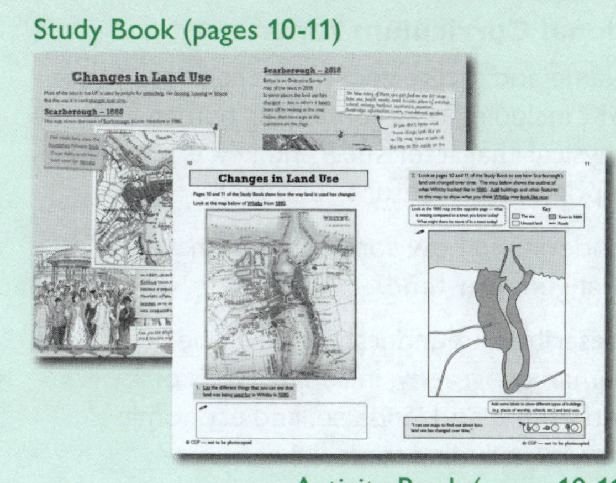

Activity Book (pages 10-11)

National Curriculum Aims
- Describe land use patterns in the UK.
- Understand how land use patterns in the UK have changed over time.
- Use maps to describe features of land use.

Introduction

This topic provides the opportunity to discuss why there have been changes in land use in the UK, such as the need for more housing around urban areas due to a growing population.

Land use in the UK has changed considerably over time. For example, the proportion of land in England that was forested declined from 15% in the 11th century to just 5% by the beginning of the 20th century — many trees were cut down for timber, and often the land was then used for agriculture. Urban land use rose during the Industrial Revolution as more people moved to work in cities.

Answers to Activity Book Questions

1. houses, railway station, gardens, public baths, library, museum, hotels, roads, farming (fields), industry (mill, warehouse, gas works, quarry), hospital, church, abbey, etc.

2. Any appropriate drawing. Compared to the map from 1880, the pupils' maps should include more roads, a larger area of housing, and less unused land to show that the town has grown. More able pupils may show changes in economic activities, such as fewer industries like mills and more tourist attractions.

Extra Activities

- As a class, discuss pupils' ideas about how the land in their own area was used in the past. Their predictions can be checked by visiting the National Library of Scotland's online resource 'Georeferenced Maps Spy Viewer' — this can be used to compare modern satellite images of an area with old Ordnance Survey® maps. In pairs, pupils can use this resource to study a particular town, city or village and note down any changes in land use. (They should use an old map which has a sensible scale and covers a date range including the year 1900.)

- Find a local newspaper story about a proposed building project in the local area (e.g. housing estate, cinema, office buildings). Ask pupils to discuss in groups whether they think the changes will improve the local area or not (e.g. bringing in more money, jobs, housing and leisure activities, but could affect wildlife and create noise/traffic). They could then each write a persuasive letter to the council, either for or against the proposal. If a local project can't be found, pupils could discuss the pros and cons of a hypothetical project, for example turning a park into a housing estate.

- Split the class into groups and give them a map of their local settlement. Ask them to identify which parts of the land they think are being used well and which parts could be improved. They can then redesign their settlement and draw a new map to show their plan, including a key to show the different buildings and land use. They could then give a short presentation about their map to the rest of the class.

North Eastern England

Study Book (pages 12-13)

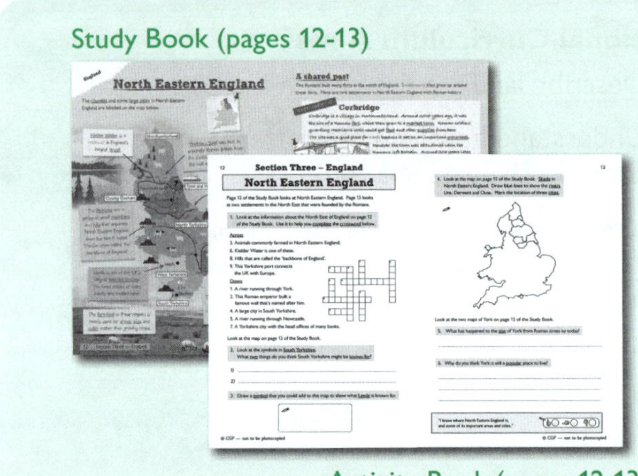

Activity Book (pages 12-13)

National Curriculum Aims

- Name and locate geographic regions of the UK, including their identifying human and physical characteristics, and key topographical features of the UK.

- Understand how some of these have changed over time.

- Describe and understand key aspects of human geography, including types of settlement and land use, and economic activity including trade links.

Introduction

North East England contains a huge variety of landscapes and has a rich history. After the Romans left Britain in the 5th century, much of England was invaded and settled by North German tribes, including the Angles, who settled in the North East. Christianity spread through the UK from early in the 7th century, when England was divided into several Anglo-Saxon kingdoms, including Northumbria in the north. Vikings raided the island of Lindisfarne in 793 AD (off the coast of Northumberland), attacking the monastery there. In the following 300 years there were many more Viking attacks. For a time, the Vikings settled in England, with York (then Jorvik) as their capital. The Viking occupation of England ended in 1066 with the battle of Stamford Bridge (close to York), just a few weeks before the Battle of Hastings and the Norman conquest of England.

Answers to Activity Book Questions

1. Across: 3 Pigs, 6 Reservoir, 8 Pennines, 9 Hull   Down: 1 Ouse, 2 Hadrian, 4 Sheffield, 5 Tyne, 7 Leeds

2. Mountains, making cutlery (stainless steel)

3. Any appropriate symbol for finance and banking, e.g. a pound sign, a coin, or a picture of a bank.

4. Any appropriate drawing with the right area shaded, the three rivers correctly shown and three cities in the area correctly marked.

5. It has become a lot bigger.

6. Any appropriate answer, e.g. it has lots of jobs/lots of things to do/good transport links/lots of houses.

Extra Activities

- Provide pupils with maps of North East England that show land use. Ask them to look for national parks, Areas of Outstanding Natural Beauty (AONBs), farmland and urban areas. They could use the map to work out the approximate proportion of the North East that each of these land uses takes up. They could then choose a way to display their data (e.g. pie chart, bar chart). Similar charts could be made for other parts of the UK so that pupils can compare land use in different regions.

- Show pupils one of J.M.W. Turner's atmospheric paintings of the North East landscape, such as "*High Force, Fall of the Tees*" or "*Malham Cove*". Get pupils to produce their own painting of a natural feature in the North East (e.g. the North Pennines) or of a man-made feature (such as the Angel of the North).

- Ask pupils to work in small groups to research a tourist attraction in the North East (e.g. Hadrian's Wall, Whitby Abbey, the Yorkshire Dales). Ask them to write and act out a television advert to attract tourists to come to that place. The advert could include information about what you can see when you visit and directions to the attraction.

South Eastern England

Study Book (pages 14-15)

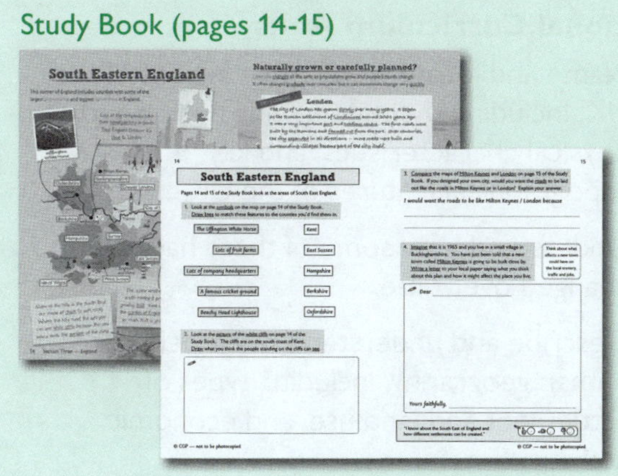

Activity Book (pages 14-15)

National Curriculum Aims

- Name and locate geographic regions of the UK, including their identifying human and physical characteristics, and key topographical features of the UK.

- Describe and understand key aspects of human geography, including types of settlement and land use, and economic activity including trade links.

Introduction

The south and east of England are home to several of the newest towns in the UK. Many of these were influenced by the garden city movement of the late 19th and early 20th centuries, which initially envisioned creating circular towns with radial roads, all surrounded by a greenbelt. Milton Keynes doesn't follow the traditional layout of a garden city, but the plans did incorporate large areas of parkland and woodland. South Eastern England also has several of the oldest settlements of the UK, such as Abingdon, Thatcham and London. For example, Abingdon was a fortified settlement in the Iron Age, prior to the invasion of Britain by the Romans.

Answers to Activity Book Questions

1. The Uffington White Horse — Oxfordshire, Lots of fruit farms — Kent, Lots of company headquarters — Berkshire, A famous cricket ground — Hampshire, Beachy Head Lighthouse — East Sussex

2. Any appropriate drawing. Pupils may include the English Channel, ferries and other boats, and possibly the coast of France.

3. Any appropriate answer, e.g. *I would want the roads to be like* Milton Keynes, *because* the grid pattern of the roads means the traffic should flow better.

4. Any appropriate letter, which includes either positive or negative effects, or a mixture, that the new town could have (e.g. more traffic, more jobs, more pollution, improved roads).

Extra Activities

- Divide the class into groups and allocate each group a county of South East England. Ask each group to research their county (using reference books or the internet) to make a fact file. This could include major landmarks, industries in the county, physical geography, population size or notable people. The shape of the counties could be cut out of coloured paper so that pupils can make their fact files in the shape of their county. These could then be combined as a wall display.

- Discuss with the class why the south of England is on average warmer than the north. This could include a discussion of the reasons why their climates might be different, such as the difference in distance to the equator, and that rain and wind most frequently come towards the UK from the direction of the Atlantic Ocean (so less rain tends to reach the South East of the country than the North West). Pupils could use a thermometer to track the temperature outside their school over the course of a week, then plot the data as a line graph. This could be compared with information about a different area of the UK from a weather website.

- Provide pupils with a map of the London Underground. Ask them to use the map to plan three routes — from King's Cross to Oxford Circus, from Paddington to Tower Hill, and from Oakwood to Elephant and Castle. They should use the names of stops and changes to describe their routes.

Eastern England

Study Book (pages 16-17)

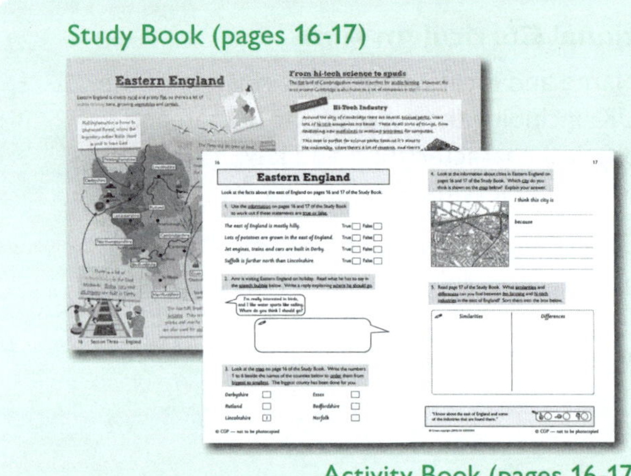

Activity Book (pages 16-17)

National Curriculum Aims

- Name and locate geographic regions of the UK, including their identifying human and physical characteristics, and key topographical features of the UK.

- Understand how some of these have changed over time.

- Describe and understand key aspects of human geography, including types of settlement and land use, and economic activity.

Introduction

This topic lets pupils look at the reasons why businesses and industries choose certain locations. It provides the opportunity to discuss the needs of different industries, such as transport, land, people and energy. There are also challenges associated with the growth of industries in certain areas. For example, there is high demand for housing in Cambridge as the number of people working in the area grows.

Answers to Activity Book Questions

1. False — True — True — False

2. Any appropriate answer, e.g. I think you should go to the Norfolk Broads because there is lots of wildlife there, and you can also do water sports like sailing there.

3. Derbyshire — 4, Rutland — 6, Essex — 3, Bedfordshire — 5, Norfolk — 2

4. *I think this city is* Cambridge *because* there is a large science park on the map.

5. Similarities — e.g. use flat land/open space, employ lots of people
   Differences — e.g. work is high paid/full-time in hi-tech industries and low paid/seasonal in fen farming. Hi-tech industries are located there because it's close to the university and fen farming is located there because of the soil.

Extra Activities

- Show pupils a topographic map of Norfolk and discuss as a class what they think will happen if the sea level rises. Find an interactive map online that shows the effects of sea level rise, then use the map to show pupils what happens to the coast of Norfolk if the sea level rises to see if their predictions were correct. They can then work in small groups to come up with some suggestions for how to prevent some of the problems that could occur, which could include sea defences, moving people to different areas and reducing carbon emissions to try to combat sea level rises.

- Ask pupils to look at the industries listed on pages 16-17 of the Study Book and make a list of the reasons why these industries are in the east of England (e.g. transport links, soil quality, people with the right skills).

- Parts of Sherwood Forest are ancient woodland. Many thousands of years ago (in the Stone Age) the majority of the UK was covered by woodland. Now it covers just 13%. Ask pupils why people might want to cut down woodland (for timber, and to clear space for farmland and towns). Discuss what they think the negative and positive effects of woodland clearance might be. The Woodland Trust campaign to restore ancient woodland and to protect and grow the UK's woodland areas. They can provides tree packs for schools — if your school has a suitable location, plant one or more trees native to the UK in the school ground. Pupils can take it in turns to be responsible for the weeding and watering throughout the year.

South West England

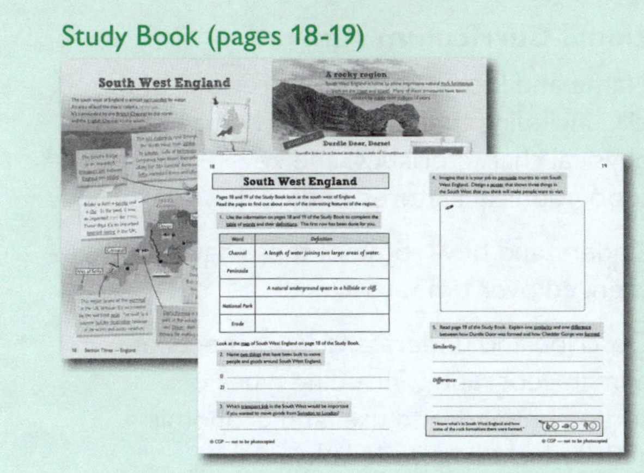

Study Book (pages 18-19)

Activity Book (pages 18-19)

National Curriculum Aims

- Name and locate geographic regions of the UK, including their identifying human and physical characteristics, and key topographical features of the UK.

- Describe and understand key aspects of human geography, including types of settlement and land use, and economic activity including trade links.

- Describe and understand key aspects of physical geography.

Introduction

The south west of England is home to some plant and animal species that are not found elsewhere in the UK. The Lizard Peninsular in Cornwall is the only place in Britain where Cornish heath grows and Britain's rarest spider is only found near Plymouth. The sub-tropical climate in the south west of England means that several tropical plants, such as palm trees, are able to grow there. As such, there are many tropical gardens throughout the area.

Answers to Activity Book Questions

1. *Peninsula* — An area of land almost surrounded by water. *Cave* — *A natural underground space in a hillside or cliff.* *National Park* — A protected area of nature. *Erode* — gradually wear something away.

2. M4, Severn Bridge

3. The M4

4. Any suitable drawing with attractions in the south west of England, e.g. Dartmoor/Exmoor with ponies, beaches in Cornwall.

5. Similarity: e.g. both were formed by water eroding limestone rocks over long periods of time. Difference: e.g. Durdle Door was formed by sea water, but Cheddar Gorge was formed by a river. / Different rock formations were made in the two places.

Extra Activities

- Ask pupils to each choose a rock formation in the UK to research, such as Lulworth Stair Hole, the Isle of Staffa, Skrinkle Haven arch, Malham Cove and Brimham Rocks. Ask pupils to draw a picture of their rock formation. The pictures can be made into a classroom display — pupils could use pins to mark the locations of their rock formations on a large map of the UK on the wall, then connect each drawing to the pin that marks its location using a piece of wool or string.

- Show pupils pictures of the Severn Bridge and ask them to estimate how long it is (1600 m). They can then look at pictures of some other long bridges in the UK (e.g. the Forth Road Bridge and the Tay Rail Bridge), and find out how they were constructed. Get pupils to work in groups to use what they have seen to design and make their own bridges. For example, each group could have the same amounts of sticky tape, modelling clay and sheets of scrap paper. They can then see which group can build the longest bridge. The structures could be tested by seeing if they can hold a small weight (e.g. a ball of modelling clay) in the middle.

- Discuss with pupils why national parks are created and why they are important for conservation. They could then research one of the national parks in the south west of England and create a leaflet about one aspect of the park. For example, they could make a guide to some of the animals found in the park or the leisure activities you can take part in at the park.

Western England

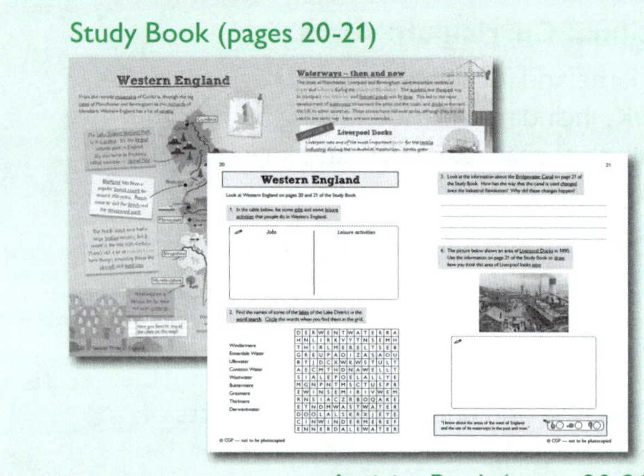

Study Book (pages 20-21)

Activity Book (pages 20-21)

National Curriculum Aims

- Name and locate geographic regions of the UK, including their identifying human and physical characteristics, and key topographical features of the UK.

- Understand how some of these have changed over time.

- Describe and understand key aspects of human geography, including types of settlement and land use, and economic activity including trade links.

Introduction

Western England played a large role during the Industrial Revolution in the UK, driven by its involvement in the textile industry. Prior to the Industrial Revolution, much of Britain's cotton was woven at home. New inventions, like the Spinning Jenny, increased the speed at which cotton could be processed and woven, enabling mass production in factories. Manchester is home to the oldest passenger train station, opened in 1830. This was on the Liverpool and Manchester railway, which was the world's first inter-city railway transporting passengers and goods.

Answers to Activity Book Questions

1. Jobs: e.g. making aircraft, making medicines, potter, tour guide, orchard farmer, working in museums, shop worker, hotel receptionist. Leisure activities: e.g. walking, climbing mountains, going to the beach, going to amusement parks, going in canal boats.

2. The locations of the lake names in the word search are shown here:

3. E.g. canals used to be used to transport lots of goods by boat. Most of this trade switched to the railways instead when they were built. The canals are now mostly used for leisure boats.

D	E	R	W	E	N	T	W	A	T	E	R	R	A
H	N	L	I	R	K	V	Y	T	N	S	E	M	H
T	H	I	R	L	M	E	R	E	L	T	S	E	B
G	R	E	U	P	A	O	I	Z	A	S	A	O	U
R	T	J	D	C	X	W	K	W	S	T	U	L	T
A	E	C	M	T	H	D	N	A	W	E	L	L	T
S	I	A	L	E	P	O	E	L	A	L	L	Y	E
M	G	N	P	N	T	M	S	C	T	U	S	P	R
E	W	I	N	S	E	M	I	R	I	V	W	E	M
R	N	S	I	A	C	Z	R	B	O	Q	A	K	E
E	T	N	D	M	W	A	S	T	W	A	T	E	R
D	O	O	L	A	L	S	K	R	X	J	E	Y	E
C	I	N	W	I	N	D	E	R	M	E	R	E	F
E	N	N	E	R	D	A	L	E	W	A	T	E	R

4. Any appropriate drawing. Pupils' drawings may include fewer boats and new leisure areas with hotels, shops, museums and restaurants.

Extra Activities

- Split pupils into teams and give each team a set of cards with key words associated with Western England (e.g. textiles, Scafell Pike, orchards). Within teams, pupils take turns to describe the word on a card without using the word itself to the rest of their team. The team that guesses the most key words correctly in one minute wins.

- Show pupils Blackpool on a map and ask them to discuss why it is a popular tourist destination, e.g. it is coastal and close to major cities. They could then look at a map to find various attractions in Blackpool, such as the Blackpool Tower, Blackpool Pleasure Beach, the Sandcastle Waterpark, Blackpool Illuminations and the Central Pier. Pupils could compare it with another seaside resort, either in the UK or abroad, and write a persuasive argument as to which place they would prefer to visit.

- Divide the class into small groups and give each group the name and height of a mountain in the Lake District. Ask them to make a simple scale model of their mountain. For example, they could make a 2D model by drawing the outline of the mountain on card and cutting it out, or make a 3D model of it in papier-mâché. Pupils could draw lines on their creations to represent contours (1 contour for each 100 m). You could use their work to make a classroom display about the mountains of the Lake District.

Southern Scotland

Study Book (pages 22-23)

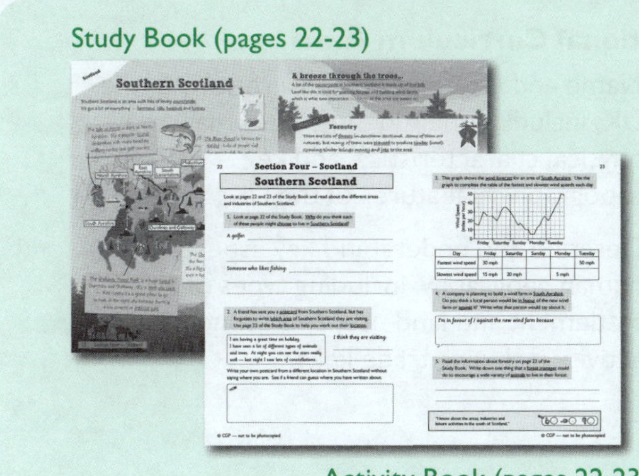

Activity Book (pages 22-23)

National Curriculum Aims

- Name and locate geographic regions of the UK, including their identifying human and physical characteristics, and key topographical features of the UK.

- Describe and understand key aspects of human geography, including types of settlement and land use, and economic activity.

Introduction

This topic provides the opportunity to discuss the region of Southern Scotland with pupils. It can also be used to start a discussion about different types of pollution. For example, wind energy can be linked to the problems of greenhouse gases and Galloway Forest Park could be used to discuss how artificial lighting can cause light pollution.

Answers to Activity Book Questions

1. *A golfer*: e.g. there are golf courses on the Isle of Arran in Southern Scotland, so the golfer would be able to play golf whenever they wanted.
   Someone who likes fishing: e.g. there are salmon in the River Tweed, so someone who likes fishing would be able to catch them there.

2. Galloway Forest Park/Dumfries and Galloway
   Any appropriate answer. Pupils could draw on information from the Study Book, e.g. they might say that they have been fishing and hillwalking to indicate the Scottish Borders, or playing golf for the Isle of Arran.

3. Fastest speeds: 35 mph, 30 mph, 25 mph. Slowest speeds: 10 mph, 20 mph

4. Any appropriate answer, e.g. *I'm in favour of the new wind farm because* wind energy is good for the environment / wind turbines don't release greenhouse gases.
   I'm against the new wind farm because I think wind turbines will change/spoil the landscape.

5. Any appropriate answer, e.g. they should make sure there are trees of different types/different ages.

Extra Activities

- Read pupils a poem by Robert Burns that talks about a landscape in Southern Scotland (e.g. The Banks of Nith, or Sweet Afton). Explain that he was from Southern Scotland (born in Ayrshire) and he liked to write about what he saw. Ask pupils to write their own poem about a local landscape that they like.

- Show pupils a map showing the average wind speeds across the UK (colour coded maps can be found online). Ask them which countries and areas of the UK are the windiest, and discuss why some areas are windier than others (e.g. the west coast is windy because the prevailing winds in the UK are westerly and southwesterly). Give pupils the locations of some of the large onshore wind farms in the UK and ask them to plot the locations on a UK map. They can then compare this map with the wind speed map and discuss why the wind farms have been built in those places.

- Discuss with pupils why Galloway Forest Park is a dark sky park (it's one of the darkest places in the UK as it's far from any big settlements). Provide pupils with maps of a few easily recognisable constellations. When a clear night is forecast, ask them go (or look) outside after dark and estimate how many stars are visible and what constellations they can see. Afterwards, discuss why they could or couldn't see stars (e.g. artificial light).

Central Scotland

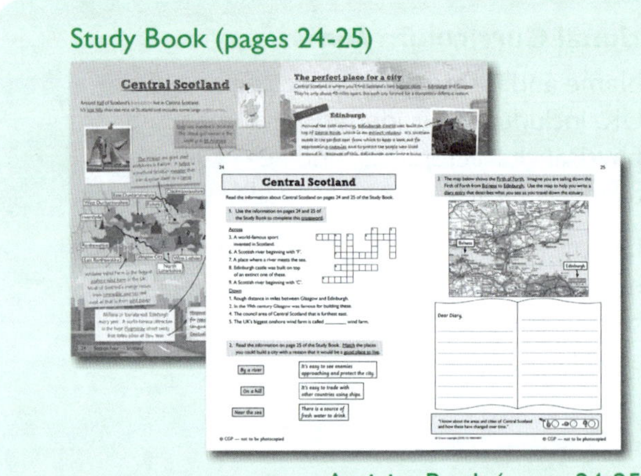

Study Book (pages 24-25)

Activity Book (pages 24-25)

National Curriculum Aims

- Name and locate geographic regions of the UK, including their identifying human and physical characteristics, and key topographical features of the UK.

- Describe and understand key aspects of human geography, including types of settlement and land use, and economic activity including trade links.

Introduction

The words firth and fjord are both derived from the same word in Old Norse, and describe the same type of landscape — long inlets of the sea formed by glaciers. The Firth of Forth has many islands along its length, which have been used for various purposes. Bass Rock was used to imprison political and religious prisoners during the 17th century, Inchkeith was used to quarantine people suffering from the plague, and several islands had gun emplacements installed to defend against enemy ships in WWI and WWII.

Answers to Activity Book Questions

1. Across: 3 — Golf, 6 — Forth, 7 — Estuary, 8 — Volcano, 9 — Clyde
   Down: 1 — Forty, 2 — Ships, 4 — Fife, 5 — Whitelee

2. By a river — There is a source of fresh water to drink. On a hill — It's easy to see enemies approaching and protect the city. Near the sea — It's easy to trade with other countries using ships.

3. Any appropriate answer that refers to things shown on the map, e.g. castles, bridges, lighthouses, beaches, islands, towns/cities, wildlife, etc.

Extra Activities

- On an interactive whiteboard, show pupils a map and pictures of the Firth of Forth. Ask them to work in pairs to think of two other places they know where the land meets the sea and list the things that can be seen there (e.g. cliffs, sandy beaches, pebble beaches, rocks, docks, harbours). Then ask them to make a PowerPoint® presentation (or a poster) about these places with a description of each one.

- Show pupils pictures of the The Kelpies sculptures in Falkirk. Tell them that The Kelpies were chosen as sculptures because they are super-strong mythological beasts, so they are a good symbol of the industrial past of the area and the strength of its communities. They are made of steel, as steelmaking was an important industry in the area. Get pupils to make small sculptures (or draw a sculpture they would make) that represent their area. They can explain to the class why they've chosen their subject and materials.

- After they have read page 25 of the Study Book, ask pupils what they know about Glasgow once being an important port for trade between the UK and the USA. Provide pupils with a map of the world and ask them to mark on Glasgow and New York and to draw a line showing the route that ships may have taken between the two. Tell pupils that today the USA imports a lot of goods from China, Japan and Germany. Ask pupils to mark Los Angeles (USA's biggest port) on their world map, as well as Bremerhaven in Germany, the Port of Shanghai in China, and Tokyo Port in Japan. Get them to draw lines joining each of these countries with either New York or Los Angeles. They could go on to research what products are traded between these countries and the USA.

Northern Scotland

Study Book (pages 26-27)

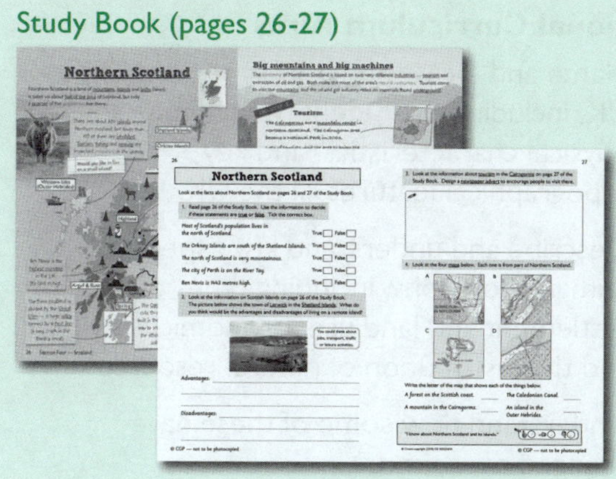

Activity Book (pages 26-27)

National Curriculum Aims

- Name and locate geographic regions of the UK, including their identifying human and physical characteristics, and key topographical features of the UK.

- Describe and understand key aspects human geography, including types of settlement and land use, economic activity, and the distribution of natural resources including energy.

Introduction

This topic lets pupils think about life on the mainland of Northern Scotland and its surrounding islands. There are many islands throughout Scotland that were inhabited in the past, but were abandoned due to the difficulties of life on those islands. For example, the island of Hirta in the St Kilda archipelago (west of the Western Isles) was inhabited from prehistoric times until evacuation in 1930. The people living there farmed the land, but a large part of their diet was the eggs and meat of sea birds on the island. A declining population, difficulties in health care and food shortages led to the last 36 islanders deciding to evacuate to the mainland in 1930.

Answers to Activity Book Questions

1. False — True — True — True — False

2. Any appropriate answer, e.g. *Advantages*: it's got nice views and lots of places to walk / there wouldn't be too much noise or traffic / there might be interesting wildlife to see. *Disadvantages*: it's far away from other places and might be hard to travel / there might not be a lot of jobs / it would take a long time for things (like parcels) to get there in bad weather / you might have to travel a long way to get medical treatment.

3. Any appropriate advert, which could include text and/or drawings of mountains, walking, skiing or wildlife.

4. *A forest on the Scottish coast* — D. *A mountain in the Cairngorms* — A. *The Caledonian Canal* — B. *An island in the Outer Hebrides* — C.

Extra Activities

- Ask pupils to look at the map on page 26 of the Study Book and discuss where would be a good place to build a hotel. Get them to list the factors that would make it a success (e.g. near to a place of interest like the Cairngorms, Loch Ness, Ben Nevis, or close to a city). Working in groups, pupils should name their hotel and make an advertising leaflet with a map and directions. It could also include information about things to do in the local area.

- Show pupils a video about how oil is extracted, and another about Scotland's wind farms. Ask them to take notes on both things. As a class, they can then discuss what they have learnt from the two videos. Get pupils to write a report comparing the advantages and disadvantages of wind power and oil.

- Get pupils to choose an island around Northern Scotland and compare it to where they live. For example, they could look at differences in climate, landscape, jobs, people, transport. They could then write a diary entry of how they might spend a day if they visited their chosen island.

- Play pupils "An Orkney Wedding, with Sunrise" by Peter Maxwell Davies. Ask them to make their own music to capture the sounds of either a place in Scotland or the place they live. For example, they could use woodblocks to make the sounds of footsteps and whistles to make the sounds of birdsong.

South Wales

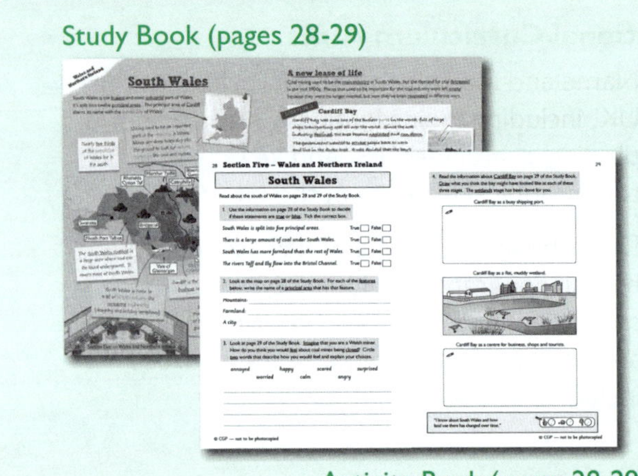

Study Book (pages 28-29)

Activity Book (pages 28-29)

National Curriculum Aims

- Name and locate geographic regions of the UK, including their identifying human and physical characteristics, and key topographical features of the UK.

- Describe and understand key aspects of human geography, including types of settlement and land use, economic activity, and the distribution of natural resources.

- Understand how some of these have changed over time.

Introduction

Around 61% of the total population of Wales live in the 12 principal areas of South Wales — around 1.9 million people in 2017. Population density was highest in Cardiff, with around 2500 people per km^2. This is still lower than the density seen in some other UK cities, such as London and Birmingham.

Answers to Activity Book Questions

1. False — True — False — True

2. *Mountains* — Rhondda Cynon Taf/Merthyr Tydfil/Caerphilly/Blaenau Gwent.
    Farmland — Monmouthshire. *A city* — Newport/Cardiff/Swansea.

3. Any appropriate answer. E.g. worried and angry. I would be angry that I was going to lose my job and worried about how I would make money.

4. Any appropriate drawings. The first should show ships and docks, the last should show a lake, with shops/businesses on the waterfront.

Extra Activities

- After pupils have read page 29 of the Study Book, put them into small groups and ask them to write down any advantages and disadvantages of the coal mining industry that they can think of. You could give them a list of key words to think about — e.g. energy source/fossil fuel, jobs, danger, environment, money. Finish by having a class discussion about the advantages and disadvantages that they came up with.

- After they have read pages 28 and 29 of the Study Book, ask pupils why people might choose to visit Cardiff (e.g. to see tourist attractions, like the castle). Show the class more information about Cardiff, such as pictures of Cardiff Bay Wetlands Reserve and the Wales Millennium Centre, or show them a tourist information video about Cardiff. Then ask pupils to use a map of the city centre to plan a day's itinerary for a visitor to the city.

- If possible, take pupils on a trip to a mining museum. Pupils could prepare for the trip by looking at what was mined in their area, and what it was used for. They could also prepare questions to ask during the trip about the lives of the miners, how the mines changed over time, and any problems that mining caused. After the trip, pupils could be asked to write a report about their visit.

- Show pupils the painting *Waste Land, Tredegar, South Wales* by Nan Youngman. Ask them to choose one of the children in the painting and write a short story about them. Pupils could be encouraged to think about what the child is doing, how they feel, and where the child's parents work.

Central & Northern Wales

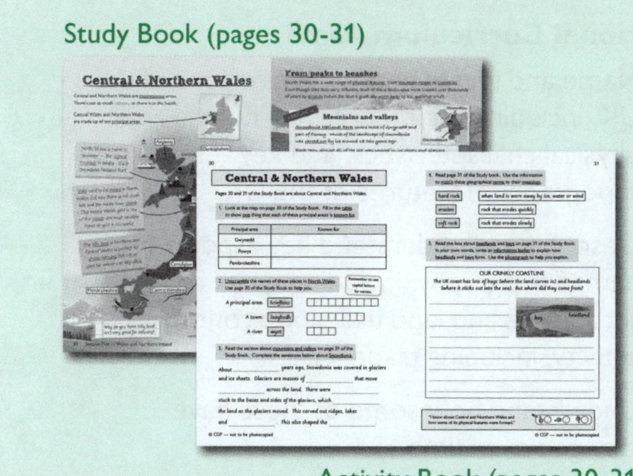

Study Book (pages 30-31)

Activity Book (pages 30-31)

National Curriculum Aims

- Name and locate geographic regions of the UK, including their identifying human and physical characteristics, and key topographical features of the UK.

- Describe and understand key aspects of human geography, including types of settlement and land use, and economic activity.

- Describe and understand key aspects of physical geography, including mountains.

Introduction

This topic allows pupils to explore how erosion can influence different landscapes. Erosion is also covered on the pages on South West England, so pupils could compare landscapes formed by coastal erosion or glacial erosion in Wales with those formed in South West England.

Answers to Activity Book Questions

1. *Gwynedd* — Gold mining/Snowdon/Mountains, *Powys* — Mountains/Sheep farming, *Pembrokeshire* — Puffins/Sheep farming/Beaches

2. Flintshire — Holyhead — Towy

3. *About* 18 000 *years ago, Snowdonia was covered in glaciers and ice sheets. Glaciers are masses of* ice *that move* slowly *across the land. There were rocks* stuck to the bases and sides of the glaciers, which eroded *the land as the glaciers moved. This carved out ridges, lakes and* valleys. This also shaped the *mountains.*

4. hard rock — rock that erodes slowly,   erosion — when land is worn away by ice, water or wind, soft rock — rock that erodes quickly

5. Pupils should explain that the land around the coast is made up of areas of soft rock and hard rock. The sea erodes the areas of soft rock quickly, forming bays. The areas of hard rock erode more slowly, so they are left as headlands, sticking out into the sea.

Extra Activities

- Give pupils a sheet of Welsh words that are commonly used in place names, and their translations (e.g. porth = port/harbour or gate, aber = river mouth or confluence, llan = parish/parish church, pont = bridge). Ask them to find place names on a map of Wales that contain these words, and work out what the names mean (if they can). Or give them all the component words, and ask them to work out what the full name of 'Llanfair PG' means.

- Show pupils a topographic map of Central and Northern Wales and ask them to discuss where they think the most people are likely to live and why (e.g. near the coast because it is less mountainous). Pupils could then look at a map of towns in the area to see if they were correct. They could then choose a town or city from the map to research and make a fact file about, which could be displayed on a large map of Wales.

- Tell pupils that rocks can be graded on their hardness using a scratch test — rocks that are harder are able to scratch those that are softer. Divide the class into groups and give each group samples of about six different types of rock (e.g. slate, granite, marble, chalk, flint and basalt). Ask them to use a scratch test to rank them from softest to hardest. (The correct order for these six would be chalk, marble, slate, basalt, granite, flint.)

Northern Ireland

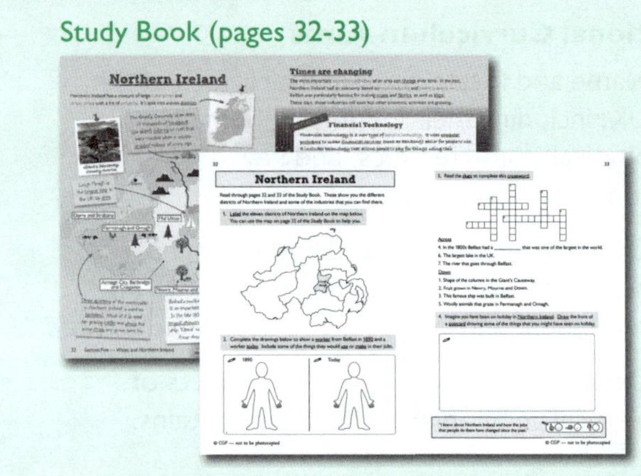

Study Book (pages 32-33)

Activity Book (pages 32-33)

National Curriculum Aims

- Name and locate geographic regions of the UK, including their identifying human and physical characteristics, and key topographical features of the UK.

- Describe and understand key aspects of human geography, including types of settlement and land use, and economic activity, including trade links.

- Understand how some of these have changed over time.

Introduction

The island of Ireland was partitioned into Northern and Southern Ireland in 1922. Following the Irish War of Independence, Southern Ireland left the UK to become the Irish Free State, whilst Northern Ireland remained part of the UK. Since then, there has been a lot of conflict in Northern Ireland, particularly 'The Troubles' from the 1960s until the 1990s. This was primarily driven by conflict between groups who either wanted Northern Ireland to remain part of the UK, or reunite with the rest of Ireland. However, in 1998, the Good Friday Agreement was signed. This agreement gave Northern Ireland its own devolved government and established councils to improve relations between Northern Irish political parties and the British and Irish governments.

Answers to Activity Book Questions

1. Pupils' labels should match the map on page 32 of the Study Book.

2. Any appropriate drawings showing a worker from 1890 (e.g. a shipbuilder, ropemaker, factory worker) and a worker from today (e.g. a business person, banker, computer programmer, tour guide, beach lifeguard).

3. Across: 4 — shipyard, 6— Lough Neagh, 7 —Lagan, 8 — eleven
   Down: 1 — hexagonal, 2 — apples, 3 — Titanic, 5 — sheep

4. Any suitable drawing showing some things that you might see whilst on holiday in Northern Ireland, e.g. The Giant's Causeway, Lough Neagh, ships in Belfast, orchards, etc.

Extra Activities

- Show pupils the locations of the Giant's Causeway and the Isle of Staffa in Scotland. Show them pictures of the rocks in both places and ask them what is similar (i.e. the rocks are hexagonal columns of basalt in both places). Show pupils a video on how the Giant's Causeway was formed and ask them to take notes. They can then use their notes to write a tourist information leaflet on the formation of the Giant's Causeway.

- Read pupils the legend of Finn McCool and how he created the Giant's Causeway and Lough Neagh. Ask pupils to draw pictures illustrating the different parts of the story (they could work alone or in small groups). They can then make their pictures into a class book that retells the legend.

- Ask pupils why they think some places share the same name (e.g. York and New York, Wales and New South Wales). Tell them that there are around 100 places named Newcastle in the world and show them where some of them are on a map (e.g. Newcastle upon Tyne, New South Wales in Australia, St Kitts and Nevis, Maine, Texas and Wyoming in the USA). Ask pupils to choose one of the places called Newcastle around the world and make an A4 poster that compares it to Newcastle in Northern Ireland. They could compare the population, climate, industries, etc. These could be used to make a class display.

Where Do You Live? – 1

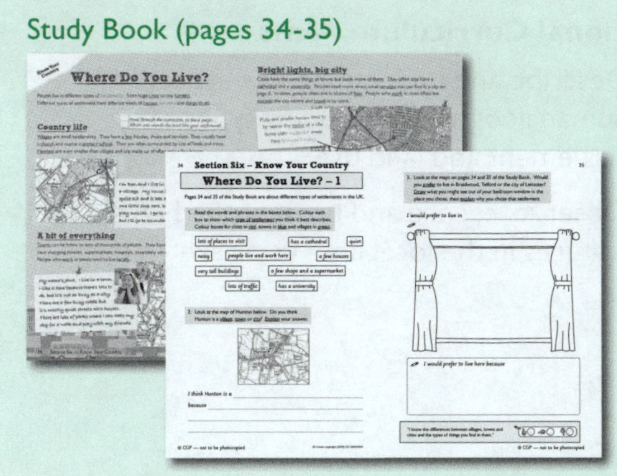

Study Book (pages 34-35)

Activity Book (pages 34-35)

National Curriculum Aims

- Describe and understand key aspects of human geography, including types of settlement and land use.

- Use maps to describe features studied.

Introduction

These pages cover some of the different types of settlement that are found in the UK, and the differences and similarities between them. Pupils are likely to have some knowledge of the type of settlement they live in.

As a warm-up activity before doing the questions in the Activity Book, ask pupils to work in pairs and discuss whether they live in a hamlet, village, town or city. They should make a list of the reasons for their choice.

Answers to Activity Book Questions

1. Village — quiet, a few houses
    Town — a few shops and a supermarket, people live and work here
    City — lots of places to visit, noisy, has a cathedral, very tall buildings, lots of traffic, has a university

2. E.g. *I think Hunton is a* village, *because* there are very few houses and few services or shops.

3. Any appropriate drawing that matches the settlement the pupil has chosen. Pupils may give any sensible reason for choosing that settlement.

Extra Activities

- Provide each pupil with a blank map of the UK and ask them to mark where they think their settlement is. Pupils could be provided with clues (e.g. whether it is in the north/west/south/east of the UK, if it is near mountains or the coast, etc). Reveal the correct location, then ask pupils to add this to their map and discuss how close they were to the correct location. Pupils can then come up with ideas for how they can remember the location in future (e.g. in relation to the shape of the coastline).

- As a class, list the names of towns, cities and villages that surround the settlement where they go to school. Ask pupils to plan a journey using a map of the region. It should start and end at the school and travel through one city, at least two towns and at least three villages. They should draw their route on the map and make some brief notes about how they would travel.

- Get pupils to use the internet and a map of the local area to make a fact file about their settlement. This could include population size, places of interest nearby, geographic features that are in or close to the settlement (e.g. rivers, mountains, coast) and transport links. Choose a settlement in a non-European country for them to make comparisons with. This could include pupils watching a video about the chosen location and taking notes. Potential cities to use include San Francisco and Buenos Aires. Alternatively, if pupils live in a very small settlement, they could compare it to a large UK city, such as Birmingham, Glasgow, Cardiff or Belfast.

Where Do You Live? – 2

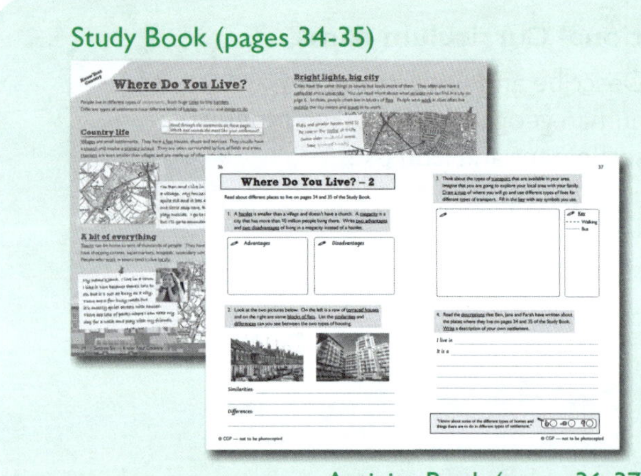

Study Book (pages 34-35)

Activity Book (pages 36-37)

National Curriculum Aims

- Describe and understand key aspects of human geography, including types of settlement and land use.

- Observe, record and present the human features in the local area using sketch maps.

Introduction

These Activity Book pages let pupils continue to explore the topic of settlement types and housing. They also encourage pupils to think about their own local area in relation to what they have learnt. Pupils can compare their own area to the settlements described in the Study Book.

Pupils will need to be provided with maps of the local area in order for them to complete question 3.

Answers to Activity Book Questions

1. Advantages: e.g. lots of jobs, lots of things to do, good transport links, lots of shops
    Disadvantages: e.g. noisy, lots of traffic, busy/lots of people, not a lot of countryside

2. Similarities: e.g. people live close together, there's not much green space.
    Differences: e.g. the flats are much taller than the terraced houses, there are separate front doors for the terraced houses, the terraced houses have parking outside and the flats don't.

3. Any appropriate drawing that includes local places to visit and different transport that can be used.
    The key should be filled in to match the map.

4. Any appropriate answer.

Extra Activities

- Discuss with pupils the area in which their school is located, such as any landmark buildings (e.g. churches, shops, interesting houses). As a class, build a 3D model to represent their settlement that can be displayed in the classroom. Assign one or two buildings in the area to each pupil, which can be added to a large map.

- Provide pupils with blank paper, clipboards, trundle wheels and/or measuring tapes and compasses. Ask them to either go around the school grounds or the inside of the school and use their equipment to make a map. The trundle wheel and measuring tape can be used to measure distances (e.g. the length and width of a playground) and the compass can be used to work out which way different parts of the map are aligned. Pupils should decide on a suitable scale for their map (e.g. 1 cm = 10 m, or 5 m, depending on the size of the school).

- Give pupils a basic street map of their local area and take them on a walking tour so that they can sketch how land is used, e.g. agriculture, retail, housing, churches. They could either use a standard map key or make up their own symbols. Alternatively, provide pupils with photos taken around the local area and see if they can identify the locations from the photographs. This can be done in groups or as a class. Provide pupils with a map of the local settlement with numbered points marked, corresponding to the locations in the photographs, then ask pupils to match each photograph to its location. More able pupils could try to work out the route the photographer took as they went around the area taking photos.

North America

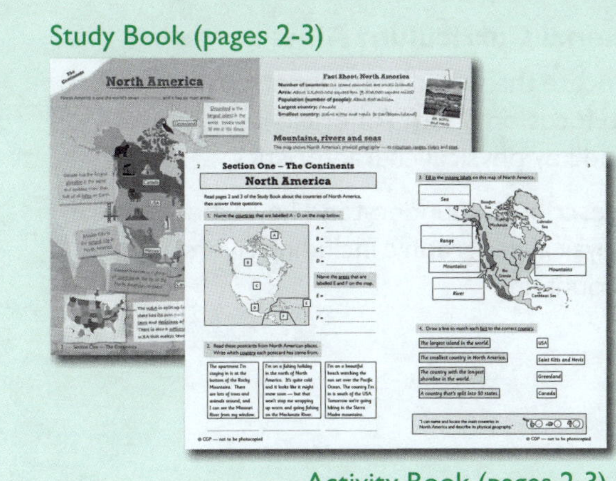

Study Book (pages 2-3)

Activity Book (pages 2-3)

National Curriculum Aims

- Locate the world's continents, using maps to focus on North America, its countries and key physical characteristics.

- Describe and understand key aspects of physical geography, including rivers and mountains.

Introduction

This topic introduces pupils to the physical geography of North America. It's the fourth most populous continent in the world after Asia, Africa and Europe. It's also the third largest continent in the world after Asia and Africa. Its size is reflected in its diversity of climates, from polar to tropical.

Before reading pages 2 and 3 of the Study Book, ask pupils if they know anything about North America already. Have any pupils ever been there or know anyone who has?

Answers to Activity Book Questions

1. A — Greenland, B — Canada, C — USA, D — Mexico, E — The Caribbean, F — Central America

2. USA, Canada, Mexico.

3. From top to bottom: Bering *Sea*, Alaska *Range*, Rocky *Mountains* (left), Appalachian *Mountains* (right), Colorado *River*.

4. The largest island in the world. — Greenland, The smallest country in North America. — Saint Kitts and Nevis, The country with the longest shoreline in the world. — Canada, A country that's split into 50 states. — USA

Extra Activities

- Pupils could make a 3D physical map of the USA. Ask them to first draw the outline of North America onto some card, then use modelling clay to create a 3D representation of the landscape using grey or brown clay for mountains, green for flat land and blue for rivers and lakes.

- Divide pupils into small groups and provide each group with a set of pictures showing the landscapes of different countries in North America. Ask them to discuss which country they think each picture could have been taken in and get them to write down their reasoning for their choices. (For younger pupils, you could provide them with a set of pictures and a set of country names and ask them to match the pictures to the names of the countries instead.)

- Ask pupils to write ten quiz questions based on their learning so far about North America. These could be true/false questions, multiple choice, or questions that need specific answers. Pupils could then test out their quiz questions in pairs or small groups.

- Tell pupils that the national government of the USA is in charge of things like printing money and defending the country. State governments are in charge of things like transport, schools and emergency services in their own states. As a class, discuss whether its a good idea for each state in the USA to have its own government.

South America

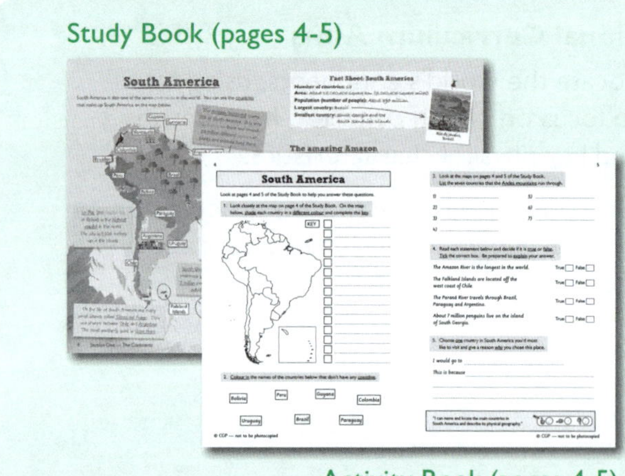

Study Book (pages 4-5)

Activity Book (pages 4-5)

National Curriculum Aims

- Locate the world's continents, using maps to focus on South America, its countries and key physical characteristics.

- Describe and understand key aspects of physical geography, including rivers and mountains.

Introduction

This topic introduces pupils to the physical geography of South America. It's the fourth largest continent in the world after Asia, Africa and North America and reaches further south than any other continent besides Antarctica. It's home to the Amazon River, which is the greatest river in the world in terms of the volume of water it carries — more than the next nine largest rivers combined.

Answers to Activity Book Questions

1. The map and the key should be coloured so that each area of the map matches the correct square in the key.

2. Pupils should have coloured in: Bolivia and Paraguay.

3. Venezuela, Colombia, Ecuador, Peru, Bolivia, Chile, Argentina.

4. False — False — True — True

5. Any appropriate answer. Pupils could draw on information from the Study Book. E.g. *I would go to* Brazil. *This is because* I like animals so I'd like to visit the rainforest. / *I would go to* Brazil. *This is because* I would like to go to the carnival. / *I would go to* South Georgia. *This is because* I'd like to see the penguins.

Extra Activities

- Ask pupils to close their Study Books and write the numbers 1-15 down the side of a piece of paper. Give pupils five minutes to see how many of the countries of South America they can remember and write down. Once the five minutes are up, pupils can check which countries (if any) they have missed. They could go on to discuss in pairs if there is any way to make the information easier to remember, for example by making up a mnemonic or a song.

- Ask pupils to draw or cut out the flags of each of the countries of South America. Call out the name of a South American country to the class. The first pupil to hold up the corresponding flag wins a point.

- Provide pupils with the population density data below which details the number of people per km² (P/km²) in each country of South America. Ask pupils to colour a blank map of South America to indicate the population density in each country. They should assign a colour to each increment from 0-10 P/km², 11-20 P/km² and so on up to 61-70 P/km² and colour each country accordingly, remembering to also create a key.
Brazil — 25 P/km², Colombia — 45 P/km², Argentina — 16 P/km², Peru — 26 P/km²,
Venezuela — 37 P/km², Chile — 25 P/km², Ecuador — 65 P/km², Bolivia — 11 P/km², Paraguay — 18 P/km²,
Uruguay — 20 P/km², Guyana — 4 P/km², Suriname — 4 P/km², French Guiana — 4 P/km²,
Falkland Islands — 0.2 P/km², South Georgia and the Sandwich Islands — 0 P/km².

Natural Americas

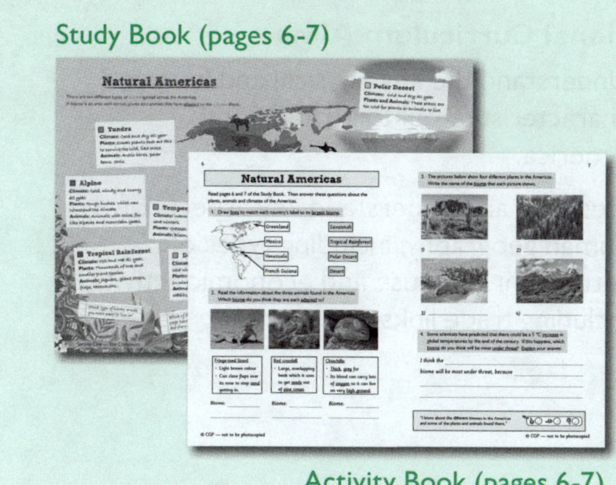

Study Book (pages 6-7)

Activity Book (pages 6-7)

National Curriculum Aims

- Locate the world's continents, using maps to focus on North and South America, their environmental regions and key physical characteristics.

- Describe and understand key aspects of physical geography, including climate zones and biomes.

Introduction

This topic introduces pupils to the climates and biomes of the Americas. The landscape varies hugely from the barren polar deserts of Greenland to the biodiverse rainforests of Brazil.

The rainforests of South America are some of the wettest places on Earth, but this continent also boasts the driest (non-polar) region in the world — the Atacama desert in Chile. The range of climates results in a huge diversity of plants and animals across the continent.

Answers to Activity Book Questions

1. Greenland — Polar Desert, Mexico — Desert, Venezuela — Savannah, French Guiana — Tropical Rainforest.

2. Fringe-toed lizard — desert, Red crossbill — coniferous forest, Chinchilla — alpine.

3. 1) Desert, 2) Coniferous forest, 3) Tundra, 4) Alpine

4. Pupils may give any biome, as long as they give sensible reasons for their answer. E.g. *I think the* tundra *biome will be most under threat, because* if the temperatures rise, the ice and snow could melt and animals would lose their habitats. / *I think the* tropical rainforest *biome will be most under threat, because* it's already hot, and if it gets even hotter, some animals might not be able to live there any more.

Extra Activities

- Ask pupils to create a piece of writing about a desert environment, e.g. a postcard, diary entry or story. Encourage pupils to describe the desert biome with reference to all five senses: touch, smell, taste, sight and sound.

- As a class, discuss with pupils which biomes would be particularly difficult to live in. Once the two most difficult biomes have been established, split the class into two teams and allocate each team one of the biomes. Each team should come up with as many reasons as they can why they think their biome would be the most difficult to live in, then engage in a class debate against the other team. Encourage pupils to develop their persuasive abilities by making their points as clear and concise as possible.

- Ask pupils to pick a biome they would like to visit, then make (or draw) a list of the things they would need to take with them if they were to travel there. Then ask them to explain their reasoning to a partner.

Moving to the Americas

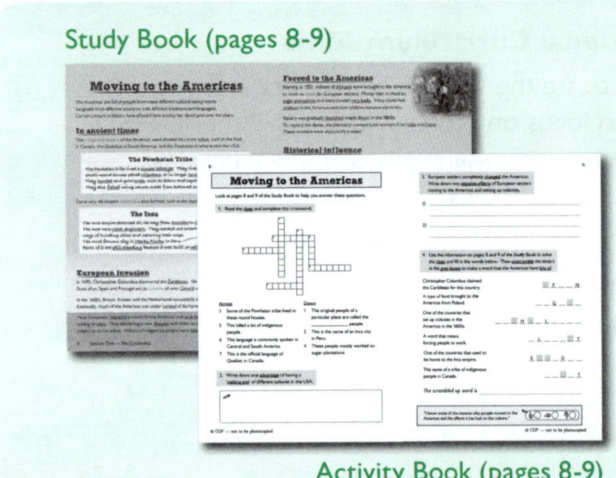

Study Book (pages 8-9)

National Curriculum Aims

- Understand the key physical and human characteristics of North and South America.

- Describe and understand key aspects of human geography, including types of settlement, land use and economic activity, including trade links.

Activity Book (pages 8-9)

Introduction

The colonisation of the Americas was a violent period in its history, from the decimation of indigenous populations to the slave trade. The celebration of Columbus Day, which commemorates the 'discovery' of the Americas by Christopher Columbus (and the beginning of colonisation), has become increasingly problematic as people consider it to be condoning the actions of European settlers against indigenous peoples. Instead, some countries and US states now observe various Indigenous People's Days on that date, to celebrate and preserve the history and culture of the people already living in the Americas prior to its so-called 'discovery'.

As a result of their troubled history, however, the Americas are now a mixture of numerous cultures. This topic covers some of the basics surrounding the Americas before colonisation, and the consequences of the arrival of European settlers for today's society.

Answers to Activity Book Questions

1. Across: 3 wigwams, 5 disease, 6 Spanish, 7 French. Down: 1 indigenous, 2 Machu Picchu, 4 slaves

2. E.g. each of the cultures has its own traditions, languages and foods. So people living in the USA get to experience lots of different cultures, which makes it an interesting place to live.

3. E.g. many people were killed in conflict/fighting / the settlers brought new diseases that harmed indigenous people / loss of indigenous cultures / the settlers brought slavery to the Americas / land was stolen from indigenous people.

4. Answers: <u>S</u>pain, bage<u>l</u>s, <u>Net</u>herlands, slave<u>r</u>y, <u>E</u>cuador, In<u>ui</u>t. Anagram: cultures.

Extra Activities

- Using the text and images on page 9 of the Study Book (and/or their own research), ask pupils to write a diary entry entitled 'A Day in the Life...' from the point of view of an African slave working in the Americas.

- Ask pupils to produce a timeline including key dates to show the developments in American history. It could include Columbus's arrival in the Caribbean in 1492, Jamaica settled by the Spanish in 1510, the first permanent English settlement in North America (Jamestown, Virginia) in 1607, the USA declaring independence from Great Britain in 1776, Mexico declaring independence from Spain in 1810, and the abolition of slavery in the USA in 1865. Encourage pupils to illustrate the timeline and add any additional important dates they know or can find out.

- Split the class into three groups. Give each group one topic to research from the languages, foods and music of the Americas. Ask each group to make a poster about their topic. The poster should include pictures and information about their chosen topic and celebrate the 'melting pot' of cultures in the Americas.

Greenland & Alaska

Study Book (pages 10-11)

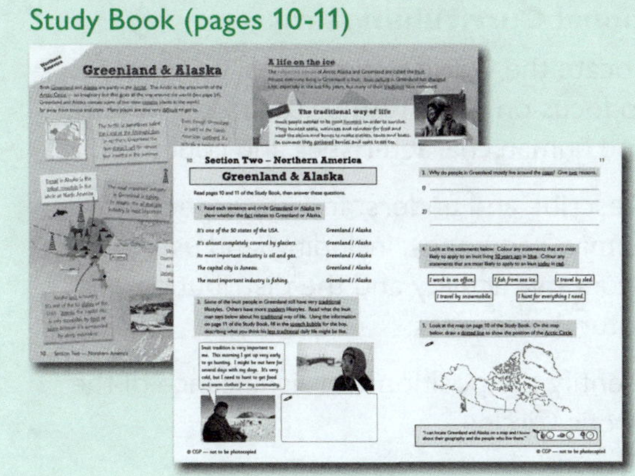

Activity Book (pages 10-11)

National Curriculum Aims

- Locate the world's continents, using maps to focus on North America, its key physical and human characteristics and countries.

- Describe and understand key aspects of human geography, including types of settlement, land use and economic activity.

- Identify the position and significance of the Arctic Circle.

Introduction

This topic introduces pupils to some of the most northerly regions of the Americas. Greenland is the least densely populated territory in the world, with a population of around 57 000. Around 18 000 people live in the capital city of Nuuk. Alaska has a population of around 740 000 and the state capital, Juneau, is home to approximately 33 000 people.

In Greenland, the population is almost entirely Inuit (88%), while in Alaska, indigenous people make up about 16% of the population. Traditional Inuit culture plays a huge role in modern-day society in Greenland in particular, but for numerous reasons, that culture is changing.

Answers to Activity Book Questions

1. Alaska — Greenland — Alaska — Alaska — Greenland

2. Any appropriate answer. Pupils should draw on information from the Study Book. E.g. "My grandfather is a very good hunter, but I don't want to be one. I've got a weekend job in a local shop. When I'm not in school or working, I hang out with my friends and drive my snowmobile."

3. E.g. Because the centre of the island is covered by glaciers. / Because fishing is an important industry, so people need to live near the sea where they can fish.

4. Pupils should have coloured blue: I fish from sea ice. / I travel by sled. / I hunt for everything I need.
   Pupils should have coloured red: I work in an office. / I travel by snowmobile.

5. Pupils' drawings should match that on page 10 of the Study Book.

Extra Activities

- Provide pupils with images of the midnight sun in Greenland. Ask pupils to use coloured pencils or paint to create their own artwork inspired by this natural phenomenon.

- Following on from question 2 in the Activity Book, pupils could work in pairs or small groups to act out a conversation between an elderly Inuit tribe member and a younger family member living in modern times. They could note the difference in day-to-day life, employment, hunting and climate conditions. Ask pupils to write out their dialogue in the form of a script and perform it to the class.

- Give pupils data on the temperature throughout the year in Nuuk and in their home location (or get them to look up this information online). Ask them to draw a line graph or a bar chart showing the average monthly temperatures of both locations. You could also ask them to write a list of the similarities and differences between the climate in both locations, looking at the trend in temperatures.

Northern and Western Canada

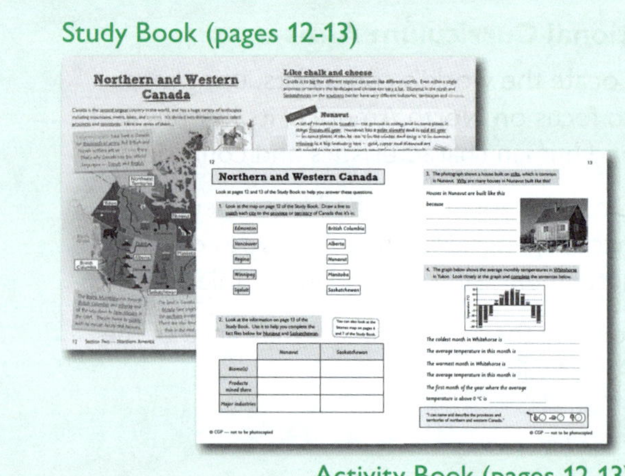

Study Book (pages 12-13)

Activity Book (pages 12-13)

National Curriculum Aims

- Locate the world's continents, using maps to focus on North America, its key physical and human characteristics and countries.

- Describe and understand key aspects of human geography, including land use, economic activity and the distribution of natural resources.

- Identify the position and significance of the Arctic Circle.

Introduction

Despite making up nearly 40% of the country's landmass, Northern Canada is home to a tiny 0.3% of the population. This is largely due to the inhospitable tundra and subarctic climates. The coldest temperature ever recorded in Canada was in the territory of Yukon in 1947, when temperatures plummeted to −63 °C. Western Canada, while still well below freezing in winter, generally experiences somewhat milder conditions. It has more farmland and contains almost a third of the population.

Answers to Activity Book Questions

1. Edmonton — Alberta,   Vancouver — British Columbia,   Regina — Saskatchewan, Winnipeg — Manitoba,   Iqaluit — Nunavut

2. Biome(s) — Nunavut: tundra,   Saskatchewan: coniferous forest and prairie/temperate grassland
   Products mined there — Nunavut: gold, copper, diamonds,   Saskatchewan: potash, uranium
   Major industries — Nunavut: mining, traditional arts and crafts,   Saskatchewan: agriculture, mining, oil production

3. E.g. *Houses in Nunavut are built like this because* lifting the houses up on stilts stops the heat from the houses defrosting the frozen ground. If the ground defrosted, the houses would sink into it.

4. *The coldest month in Whitehorse is* January. *The average temperature in this month is* −19 °C (allow −17 to −19). *The warmest month in Whitehorse is* July. *The average temperature in this month is* 14 °C (allow 12 to 14). *The first month of the year where the average temperature is above 0 °C is* April.

Extra Activities

- Have a class discussion about the challenges facing the people living in Alert (e.g. winter darkness, transport, temperature, food imports). Ask pupils how they think the people in Alert adapt to these challenges.

- Show pupils pictures of some Inuit animal carvings. Ask pupils to pick an animal they might find in the Canadian tundra (e.g. reindeer, snowy owl, Arctic fox, grizzly bear, polar bear, ringed seal, stoat, Arctic hare) and use modelling clay to sculpt a model of their chosen animal in the style of the Inuit carvings.

- Pupils could research the native animal life in Northern and Western Canada. Pupils could produce an information text in the form of a poster about one animal and present their findings to the rest of the class, using their posters to point out key facts and features. They could include information on the animal's habitat, its prey, predators and life span. Some suggestions for animals include: Arctic hare, moose, beaver, black bear, prairie dog.

Eastern Canada

Study Book (pages 14-15)

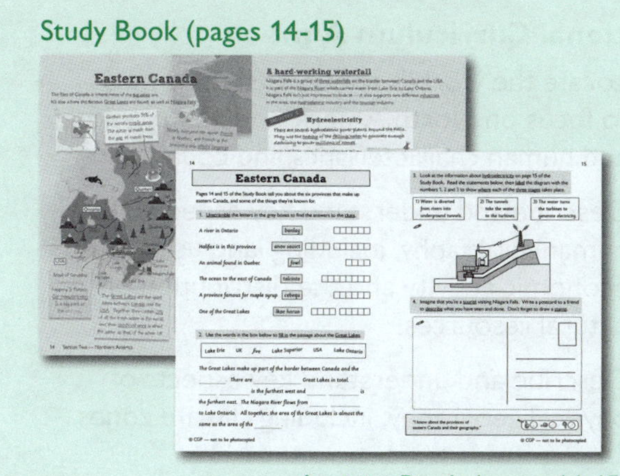

Activity Book (pages 14-15)

National Curriculum Aims

- Locate the world's continents, using maps to focus on North America, its key physical and human characteristics and countries.

- Describe and understand key aspects of human geography, including land use, economic activity and the distribution of natural resources.

Introduction

Eastern Canada only makes up about a third of the area of Canada, but contains over two thirds of the country's population. Canada's two largest cities, Toronto and Montreal, are located in this region. Ontario attracts the most tourists of any province or territory — almost double that of the next most popular destination (British Columbia).

Answers to Activity Book Questions

1. Albany — Nova Scotia — wolf — Atlantic — Quebec — Lake Huron

2. *The Great Lakes make up part of the border between Canada and the* USA. *There are* five *Great Lakes in total.* Lake Superior *is the furthest west and* Lake Ontario *is the furthest east. The Niagara River flows from* Lake Erie *to Lake Ontario. All together, the area of the Great Lakes is almost the same as the area of the* UK.

3. Pupils should have labelled the diagram as shown on the right.

4. Any appropriate answer that describes some of the things that might be seen at Niagara Falls, such as the Niagara River, the Falls themselves and thousands of tourists.

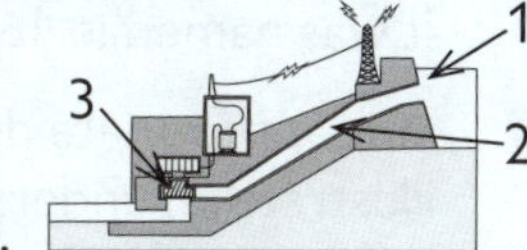

Extra Activities

- Provide pupils with the data below about the use of renewable energy sources around the world. Ask pupils to create two bar charts — the first comparing how much of each country's total electricity generation comes from renewable sources, and the second comparing how much of each country's total comes from hydropower specifically. Once pupils have completed their graphs, they can discuss how Canada compares with the rest of the world.
  Percentage of total electricity generation from renewables: Brazil — 82%, Canada — 67%, China — 26%, Costa Rica — 99%, Cuba — 5%, Finland — 46%, Spain — 40%, UK — 26%, USA — 16%
  Percentage of total electricity generation from hydropower: Brazil — 67%, Canada — 60%, China — 20%, Costa Rica — 74%, Cuba — 0%, Finland — 24%, Spain — 15%, UK — 3%, USA — 7%

- Prince Edward Island is famous for being the site of Green Gables — the farmhouse where the novel *Anne of Green Gables* is set. The novel uses a lot of detailed setting description. Read pupils a passage from the novel that focuses on the landscape and then ask pupils to draw or paint an image to show how they imagine it to look. Pupils can compare their images with those of the rest of the class to see how differently they each imagined the landscape based on the same description.

- Ask pupils to design a car to be manufactured in Ontario for use throughout the country. They should consider the different terrains and climates of Canada and design a car that would be suitable for snowy, icy, rocky and flat terrains, as well as all weathers. Ask pupils to draw a labelled diagram of their car and explain the key points of their design to the class or to a partner.

USA – East Coast

Study Book (pages 16-17)

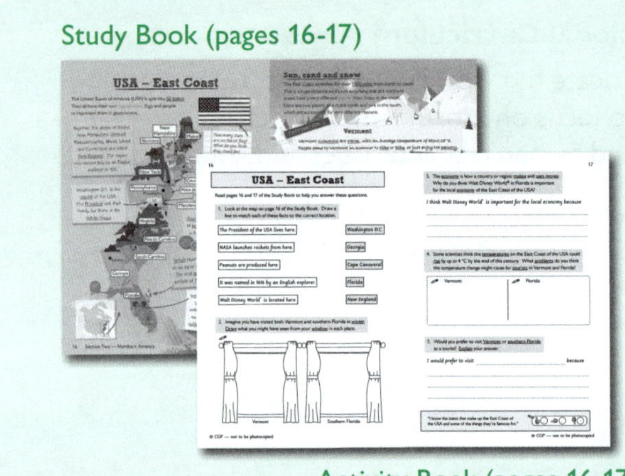

Activity Book (pages 16-17)

National Curriculum Aims

- Locate the world's continents, using maps to focus on North America, its key physical and human characteristics and countries.

- Describe and understand key aspects of human geography, including land use, economic activity and the distribution of natural resources.

- Describe and understand key aspects of physical geography, including climate zones.

Introduction

The East Coast of the USA contains much of the first land to be colonised by European settlers. Despite settlers eventually occupying the entirety of the country, the eastern states remain the most densely populated. Like Canada, the size of the USA lends itself to a great deal of diversity in terms of climates, biomes and land use. The East Coast is home to contrasting landscapes, from enormous metropolitan areas like New York City, to the 1.5 million acres (6000 km²) of flat, open wetland in the Florida Everglades.

Answers to Activity Book Questions

1. The President of the USA lives here — Washington D.C.,
   NASA launches rockets from here — Cape Canaveral,   Peanuts are produced here — Georgia,
   It was named in 1616 by an English explorer — New England, Walt Disney World® is located here — Florida

2. Any appropriate drawing. Pupils should draw on information from the Study Book. Pupils' drawings should illustrate an understanding that Vermont is very cold and often snowy in winter, while southern Florida is very mild. Pupils may wish to add other details, for example mountains and skiers in Vermont and beaches and surfers in South Florida.

3. E.g. *I think Walt Disney World® is important for the local economy because* it attracts a lot of tourists who come to the East Coast of the USA and spend money.

4. E.g. *Vermont:* it might not be as cold or snowy. / The snow could melt and people wouldn't be able to ski there any more. *Florida:* the summers might get too hot for tourists.

5. Any appropriate answer. Pupils should draw on information from the Study Book. E.g. *I would prefer to visit Vermont because* I'd like to see the leaves in autumn / it's warm in the summer but not too hot / I want to learn to ski.

Extra Activities

- Ask pupils to write and present a weather forecast for a typical winter or summer day in Vermont or southern Florida.

- Show pupils pictures of New York City's most famous skyscrapers (e.g. the Empire State Building, One World Trade Center, the Chrysler Building, 30 Rockefeller Plaza). Ask pupils to design their own skyscraper, labelling its key features. Or split pupils into small groups and ask each group to build a skyscraper out of lollipop sticks and glue. There could be a prize for the tallest (structurally sound) building.

- Pupils could research a hurricane that has hit Florida. Ask them to find out when it occurred, the damage it caused, and the primary and secondary effects it had on local people.

USA – In the Middle

Study Book (pages 18-19)

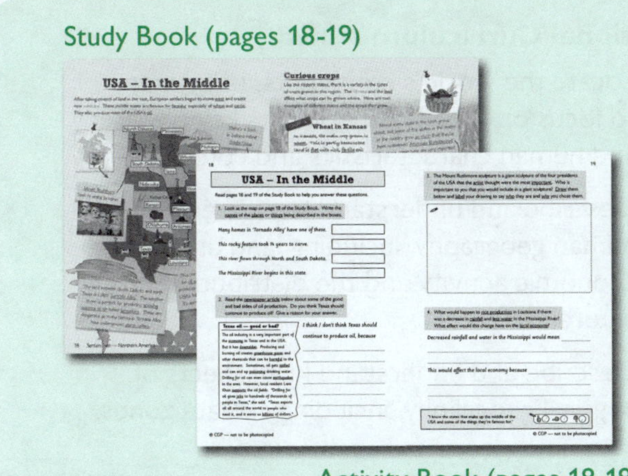

Activity Book (pages 18-19)

National Curriculum Aims

- Locate the world's continents, using maps to focus on North America, its key physical and human characteristics and countries.

- Describe and understand key aspects of human geography, including land use, economic activity and the distribution of natural resources.

- Describe and understand key aspects of physical geography, including climate zones.

Introduction

While many of the USA's biggest cities are concentrated around the coast, the states in the central USA have the highest percentage of farmland in the country. Between 70% and 90% of the land in North Dakota, South Dakota, Nebraska, Kansas and Oklahoma is covered by farmland. Agriculture plays a huge part in the economies of these states, but other industries like manufacturing and oil production also play a significant role.

Answers to Activity Book Questions

1. Storm cellars — Mount Rushmore — Missouri — Minnesota

2. Pupils may answer either way, as long as they give a sensible reason for their answer. E.g. *I think Texas should continue to produce oil, because* people all around the world use it / they have a lot of it / it creates jobs / it brings in a lot of money to the USA.
   I don't think Texas should continue to produce oil, because it's bad for the environment / drilling for oil can cause earthquakes / it can poison drinking water / producing/burning it creates greenhouse gases.

3. Any appropriate drawing. Pupils may choose any four people to feature on their sculpture, providing they give sensible reasons for their choice.

4. E.g. *Decreased rainfall and less water in the Mississippi would mean* that the ground wouldn't be regularly covered in water, so rice wouldn't be able to grow. *This would affect the local economy because* rice is one of the main crops grown in Louisiana, so if they can't grow it, they can't sell it to make money.

Extra Activities

- Provide pupils with photos or a video clip showing damage caused by a tornado in Texas. Ask pupils to imagine that they were living in 'Tornado Alley' when it happened. Ask them to write a diary entry describing what happened that day. Where were they when the tornado arrived? What happened during the tornado? Did they go into a storm cellar? How did they feel afterwards? What damage had been caused?

- Remind pupils that not all years in Louisiana experience heavy rainfall and flooding waters. Much of Louisiana was abnormally dry for the time of year in 2018. Ask pupils to research the threat of drought in Louisiana using some prompt questions: In the last decade, which years have been abnormally dry in Louisiana? What causes the change in rainfall? Pupils could use the information from their research to write a newspaper article about drought in Louisiana. It could include a description of what the impacts of a drought would be on rice production and the local economy.

- Remind pupils that every US state has a state capital. Provide them with a list of the state capitals for the states mentioned on pages 18 and 19 of the Study Book and challenge them to see how many they can learn and remember. They could make up a mnemonic or a song to help them remember as many as possible.

USA – Out West

Study Book (pages 20-21)

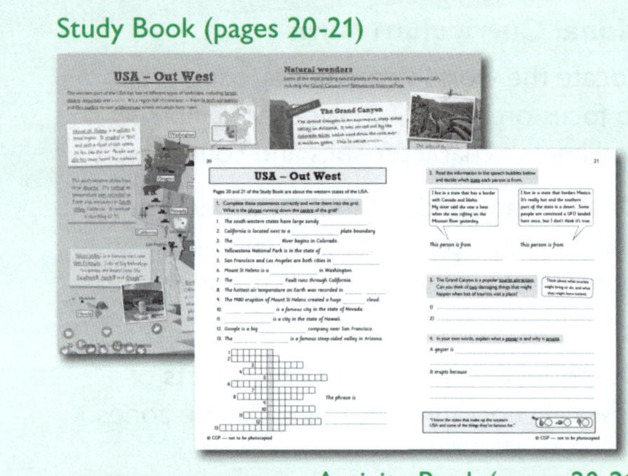

Activity Book (pages 20-21)

National Curriculum Aims

- Locate the world's continents, using maps to focus on North America, its key physical and human characteristics and countries.

- Describe and understand key aspects of human geography, including land use, economic activity and the distribution of natural resources.

- Describe and understand key aspects of physical geography, including climate zones.

Introduction

The western states are home to some of the largest cities in the country, including Los Angeles, Las Vegas and San Francisco. Despite this, much of the area is sparsely populated and is well known for its natural landmarks, such as the Grand Canyon and Yellowstone National Park. It's also the birthplace of the oldest film industry in the world — Hollywood.

Answers to Activity Book Questions

1. Deserts, tectonic, Colorado, Wyoming, California, volcano, San Andreas, Death Valley, ash, Las Vegas, Honolulu, technology, Grand Canyon. *The phrase is* Silicon Valley.

2. Speech bubble 1: *This person is from* Montana. Speech bubble 2: *This person is from* New Mexico.

3. E.g. Tourists can create litter/noise pollution/traffic jams. / Lots of people walking around the same places can disturb the wildlife/wear away the ground.

4. E.g. *A geyser is* a hole in the ground that hot water and steam come out of. *It erupts because* there's magma underground which heats up the water until it boils and bursts out of the geyser.

Extra Activities

- Ask pupils to conduct research on one of the animals that live in the west, such as bears, bison, wolves or condors. Get them to produce a fact file that includes details about the habitat of the animal, its diet and eating habits, size, appearance and the reasons why it's well suited to its environment in the west. The completed fact files could be made into a class display about the wildlife of the western USA.

- Pupils could design a board game on the subject of the USA to play in small groups. Provide pupils with a blank game board with squares numbered 1 - 100 (or get them to draw their own). The game board could be square or in the shape of the USA. Ask pupils to prepare a series of trivia question cards based on the Study Book content, then place a question card on some of the squares. Starting on square 1, players roll one or more dice to determine the number of squares they can advance. If they land on a trivia card, they must answer it correctly to remain on that square. If they answer wrongly, they have to move back three spaces. The winner is the first player to reach square 100.

- Ask pupils to compare the map of the western USA on page 20 of the Study Book with the biome map on pages 6-7. Either provide pupils with a blank map of the western states or ask them to draw one, then shade in each state to indicate the biome or biomes that cover each state. Pupils should add a key to their drawing to indicate which colour denotes which biome.

Mexico and Central America

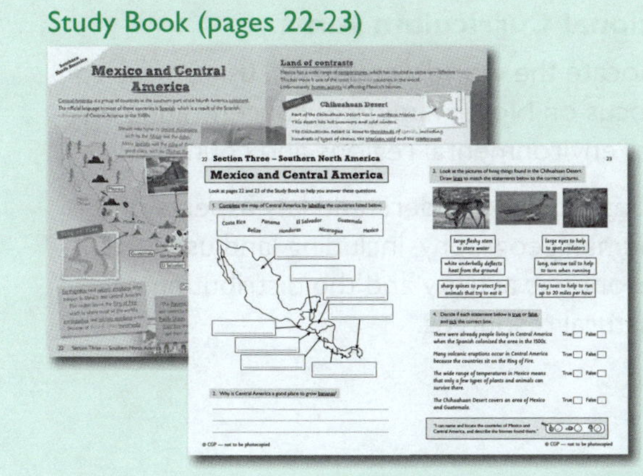

Study Book (pages 22-23)

Activity Book (pages 22-23)

National Curriculum Aims

- Locate the world's countries, using maps to focus on North America, concentrating on its environmental regions and countries.

- Describe and understand key aspects of physical geography, including climate zones and biomes.

Introduction

These pages allow pupils to explore the countries of Central America, with a focus on the biomes found in Mexico. It is estimated that around 10% of the known species of animals and plants in the world are found in Mexico, including many species that are not found elsewhere, making it one of the most biodiverse countries in the world. This is partially due to its location, as it's where the continents of North and South America join, which has allowed different species to move into Mexico from both continents.

Answers to Activity Book Questions

1. Pupils' labels should match the map on page 22 of the Study Book.

2. E.g. it has rich volcanic soil and tropical weather.

3. pronghorn — large eyes to help to spot predators, white underbelly deflects heat from the ground
   roadrunner — long, narrow tail to help to turn when running, long toes to help to run up to 20 miles per hour (pupils may also have drawn a line to 'white underbelly deflects heat from the ground')
   cactus — large fleshy stem to store water, sharp spines to protect from animals that try to eat it.

4. True — True — False — False

Extra Activities

- Ask pupils to research the Chilean earthquake of 2010. Provide them with blank maps on which to draw the location of the epicentre of the earthquake and the places that were affected by the earthquake and tsunami. In groups, ask them to create a news bulletin to read out to the class, giving key information about what has happened, the areas that have been affected and what people should do next.

- Trade is considered to be unfair when farmers (and other workers) receive a very low income and have poor living conditions whilst the businesses that sell their products make a large amount of money. The FAIRTRADE Mark is awarded to products that are sold under certain fair-trading conditions. Find a video about Fairtrade farming (e.g. of bananas) to show to the class. Ask pupils to make notes whilst watching the video, and then use what they have learned to create a poster to explain what Fairtrade is and encourage people to buy products with the FAIRTRADE Mark.

- Ask pupils to reread the information about threats to wildlife on page 23 of the Study Book. They should then choose one of the animals to research further (or choose another endangered animal from Central America). Ask pupils to use their research to create a fact file, which could include the animal's range, appearance, diet, behaviour, adaptations and why it has become endangered (useful information can be found using the IUCN Red List[©]).

The Caribbean

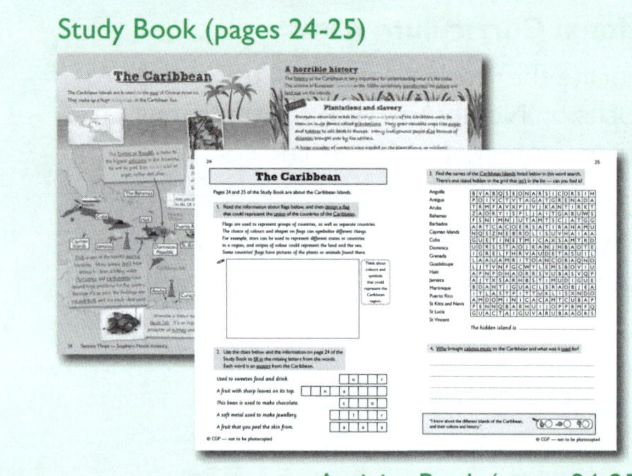

Study Book (pages 24-25)

Activity Book (pages 24-25)

National Curriculum Aims

- Locate the world's countries, using maps to focus on North America, concentrating on its environmental regions and countries.

- Describe and understand key aspects of human geography, including land use, economic activity and the distribution of natural resources.

Introduction

This topic allows pupils to think about the different people that have lived in the Caribbean over time and how European colonisation caused large amounts of change to the population and culture of the region. There is evidence of human settlement of the Caribbean from around 5000 BC, with several different tribes colonising the islands in the millennia that followed. This included the Ciboney, Taino and Kalinago (otherwise known as Island Caribs). Columbus landed in the Bahamas in 1492, leading to the European colonisation of the Caribbean and huge losses for the indigenous populations due to diseases, enslavement and warfare. Today, only around 3000 Kalinago live in the Kalinago Territory on the north eastern coast of Dominica.

Answers to Activity Book Questions

1. Any suitable drawing. Symbolism pupils could have used includes stars to represent the islands, yellow to represent coastlines/beaches, and blue to represent the Caribbean sea.

2. sugar — pineapple — cocoa — silver — banana

3. The locations of the names of the Caribbean islands in the grid are here: *The hidden island is* Montserrat.

4. Slaves brought calypso music from Africa. They used it to communicate, spread news and mock their masters because they weren't allowed to talk to one another. It also helped them to keep their culture alive.

Extra Activities

- Ask pupils to look at page 24 of the Study Book and choose three islands to research. Provide them with a table to fill in, with columns for: island name, population size, main exports, topography (landscape), capital city, plants and animals, and an interesting fact. Discuss their results as a class and compare results to find out which country has the most people and which countries have similar exports or wildlife.

- As a class, listen to some calypso music. This could include recordings of Lovey's String Band, who were the first calypso band to have their music recorded. Ask pupils how they would describe the calypso music in words. Play other music genres from the Caribbean, such as ska, rocksteady, merengue and mambo. Pupils could discuss the differences between the genres, such as the instruments used (each genre has a mix of both African and European influences — African influences include percussion instruments such as drums, and call and response phrases, while European influences include the use of instruments such as guitars).

- Ask pupils to each choose a Caribbean island to research and to look at the main foods eaten there. Each pupil could create a drawing of the national dish of their island, along with a recipe for that dish. These can then be displayed on the classroom wall to show the food eaten throughout the Caribbean.

Andean Nations

Study Book (pages 26-27)

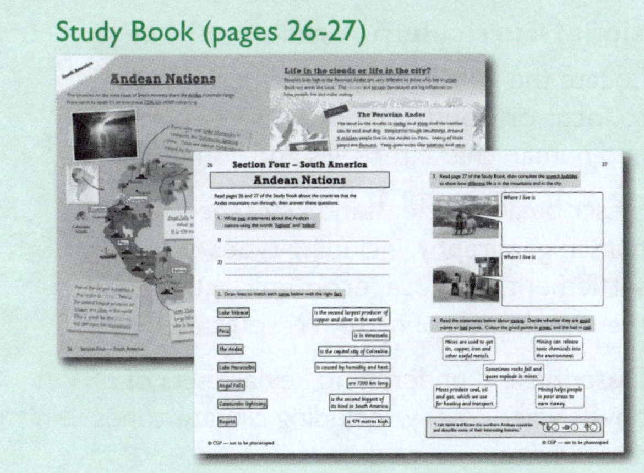

Activity Book (pages 26-27)

National Curriculum Aims

- Locate the world's continents, using maps to focus on South America, its key physical and human characteristics and countries.

- Describe and understand key aspects of human geography, including land use, economic activity and the distribution of natural resources.

- Describe and understand key aspects of physical geography, including climate zones and mountains.

Introduction

The Andes are the longest mountain range in the world, running down the west of South America from the north coast of Venezuela to the southern tip of the continent. They were formed by the Nazca tectonic plate being forced under the South American plate, thus pushing up the land to form mountains.

Answers to Activity Book Questions

1. E.g. Lake Titicaca is the world's <u>highest</u> large lake. Angel Falls is the world's <u>tallest</u> waterfall.

2. Lake Titicaca — is the second biggest of its kind in South America. Peru — is the second largest producer of copper and silver in the world. The Andes — are 7200 km long. Lake Maracaibo — is in Venezuela. Angel Falls — is 979 metres high. Catatumbo lightning — is caused by humidity and heat. Bogotá — is the capital city of Colombia.

3. Any appropriate answer. E.g. *Where I live is* cold and very hilly. My family are farmers. There aren't any shops up here, but we grow everything we need. / *Where I live is* warm and the land is flatter than in the nearby mountains. There are some shops to buy things, but it's also very crowded.

4. Pupils should have coloured green: Mines are used to get tin, copper, iron and other useful metals. / Mines produce coal, oil and gas, which we use for heating and transport. / Mining helps people in poor areas to earn money.
   Pupils should have coloured red: Sometimes rocks fall and gases explode in mines. / Mining can release toxic chemicals into the environment.

Extra Activities

- Ask pupils to research how llamas are adapted to living in the harsh conditions high in the Andes. Pupils can then draw a picture of a llama and label the features that make it well-suited to life in the mountains. Some features include: long eyelashes to protect their eyes from dust blown in the wind, a thick woolly coat to protect them from the cold, and padded feet to help them walk on rocky ground.

- Ask pupils to draw a picture of what they think the Catatumbo lightning over Lake Maracaibo would look like. Ask pupils to imagine that they are spending a night at Lake Maracaibo and write a description of what it was like. Their descriptions should include what they saw and heard, and how it made them feel.

- The Andes mountain range is 7200 km long, and its highest point at the summit of Aconcagua is almost 7000 m above sea level. Ask pupils to find out about other mountain ranges in the world, including: the Rocky Mountains, Himalayas, Alps, Karakoram, Ural Mountains, Altai Mountains, Atlas Mountains and Carpathians, and find out the length and highest point in each. Pupils can then use an atlas to identify which mountain ranges stretch across more than one country and mark them on a blank map of the world.

Brazil and the Guianas

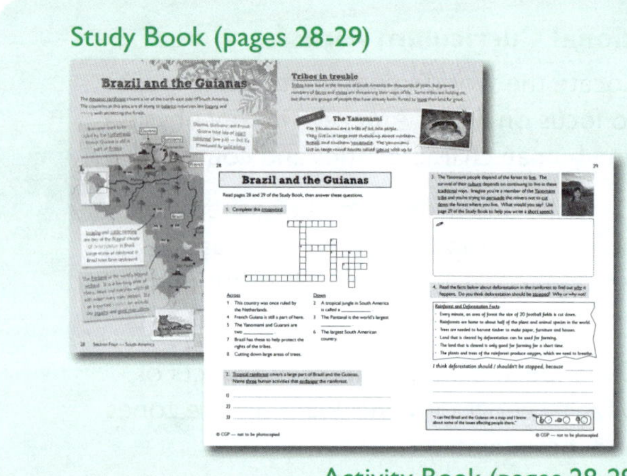

Study Book (pages 28-29)

Activity Book (pages 28-29)

National Curriculum Aims

- Locate the world's continents, using maps to focus on South America, its key physical and human characteristics and countries.

- Describe and understand key aspects of human geography, including types of settlement, land use, economic activity and the distribution of natural resources.

- Describe and understand key aspects of physical geography, including climate zones and biomes.

Introduction

The climate in Brazil varies quite dramatically from the tropical north to the temperate climate in the south. In the centre of the country is the Cerrado, a large tropical savannah region. This is the largest savannah region in South America and, like the rainforest in the north, is being degraded rapidly by farming.

Answers to Activity Book Questions

1. Across: 1 Suriname, 4 France, 5 tribes, 7 laws, 8 deforestation
   Down: 2 rainforest, 3 wetland, 6 Brazil

2. E.g. cattle farming / (gold) mining / illegal mining / logging/cutting down trees (deforestation)

3. Any appropriate answer. Pupils should draw on information from the Study Book. Pupils could reference the Yanomami's reliance on the rainforest for hunting and growing crops, and the risk of introducing new diseases to the tribe.

4. E.g. *I think deforestation should be stopped, because* it destroys the forest where lots of people, plants and animals live / it's destroying trees that make oxygen, which we need to live.
   I think deforestation shouldn't be stopped, because we need the paper and furniture that comes from the trees / the cleared land can be used for farming, which gives us food.

Extra Activities

- Explain to the class that Brazil is not entirely covered by the Amazon rainforest — the Cerrado is a large area of savannah grassland in the centre of the country, and the Atlantic Forest is an area of both wet and dry forest along the east coast of the country (said to be one of the most diverse ecosystems in the world, along with the Amazon). Ask pupils to choose one of these biomes to research. They should find out its climate, location, plant species, animal species and why the biome is threatened.

- Expanding on their answers to question 4 in the Activity Book, ask pupils to consider different opinions towards deforestation. Split pupils into four groups: environmentalists, farmers, timber merchants and people living in the rainforest. Ask pupils to think about how their group might feel about deforestation, then engage in a debate about whether or not deforestation should continue in Brazil.

- Get pupils to reread page 29 of the Study Book. Ask them to imagine that they have been made homeless by environmental changes. Why might they have had to move? How they would manage living in a tent? What they might need and what would they take with them when leaving their home? Ask pupils to create a piece of writing or a drawing to show what they think the experience would be like.

The Southern Cone

Study Book (pages 30-31)

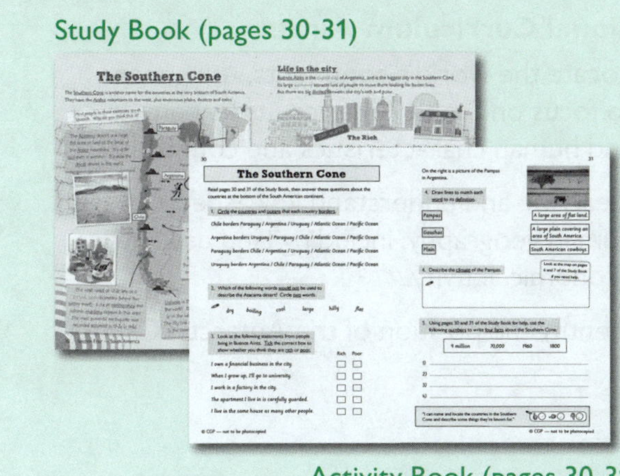

Activity Book (pages 30-31)

National Curriculum Aims

- Locate the world's continents, using maps to focus on South America, its key physical and human characteristics and countries.

- Describe and understand key aspects of human geography, including types of settlement, land use and economic activity.

- Describe and understand key aspects of physical geography, including climate zones and biomes.

Introduction

The countries of the Southern Cone aren't just grouped geographically, but have similar histories, economies and demographics. As a result of Spanish colonialism and subsequent immigration, 97% of the population of Argentina is white or mestizo (a combination of European and indigenous heritage). The numbers in the rest of the Southern Cone are similarly high — 95% in Paraguay, 89% in Chile and 88% in Uruguay. Although agriculture played a vital role in the development of the Southern Cone countries, over 84% of the population live in urban areas today.

The Southern Cone is now considered to be one of the most economically stable regions of the continent, with generally higher incomes and higher standards of living than other parts of South America.

Answers to Activity Book Questions

1. Chile — Argentina, Atlantic Ocean, Pacific Ocean,   Argentina — Uruguay, Paraguay, Chile, Atlantic Ocean, Paraguay — Argentina,   Uruguay — Argentina, Atlantic Ocean

2. Pupils should have circled: boiling and hilly.

3. Rich — Rich — Poor — Rich — Poor

4. Pampas — A large plain covering an area of South America,   Gauchos — South American cowboys, Plain — A large area of flat land.

5. E.g. The climate of the Pampas is warm in the summer and cold in the winter / temperate.

6. E.g. 9 million people in Argentina have to live on about £1.50 a day. / Around 70,000 people live in Ushuaia (the most southerly city in the world). / The most powerful earthquake ever recorded happened in Chile in 1960. / South American cowboys have kept cows on the Pampas since the 1800s.

Extra Activities

- Robinson Crusoe Island is located off the coast of Chile. It's so-called because the real-life story of a sailor marooned there is thought to be the inspiration for the story of Robinson Crusoe by Daniel Defoe. Read a summary of the story of Robinson Crusoe as a class, then ask pupils to illustrate the story in the style of a comic strip.

- Ask pupils to reread page 31 of the Study Book and show them pictures of the slums in Buenos Aires. Ask pupils to write a diary entry from the perspective of a child who lives in these conditions.

- Ushuaia is the most southerly city in the world. Provide pupils with a world map, globe or atlas and ask them to identify the most southerly cities on the other continents. Then ask them to locate the most northerly city on each continent.

The Southern Islands

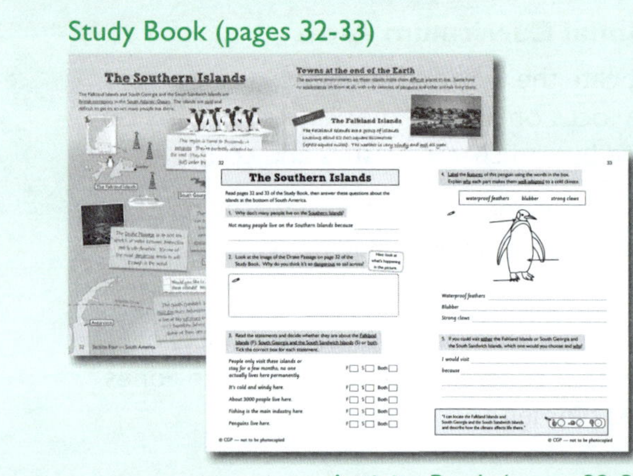

Study Book (pages 32-33)

Activity Book (pages 32-33)

National Curriculum Aims

*   Locate the world's continents, using maps to focus on South America, its key physical and human characteristics and countries.

*   Describe and understand key aspects of human geography, including land use and economic activity.

*   Identify the position of the Antarctic Circle.

Introduction

The Falkland Islands and South Georgia and the South Sandwich Islands are two British Overseas Territories. Although they're self-governing, their head of state is the British monarch and their residents are British citizens.

Answers to Activity Book Questions

1. E.g. *Not many people live on the Southern Islands because* they are difficult to get to and very cold.

2. E.g. There are thunderstorms / the sea is very rough.

3. S — Both — F — F — Both

4. E.g. *Waterproof feathers* stop penguins getting wet/cold when they swim in the sea. *Blubber* keeps penguins warm. *Strong claws* help them to grip on to the ice when they are walking.

5. Any appropriate answer. Pupils should draw on information from the Study Book. E.g. *I would visit* South Georgia and the South Sandwich Islands *because* I like snow, and I'd like to visit an active volcano.

Extra Activities

*   Explain to the class that Kennings poems describe what a person, animal or object is and does. The poems are like riddles and each line acts like a clue to help the reader work out the subject of the poem. Here is an example: Great swimmer / Seabed glider / Ocean lover / Fish consumer / Echolocation user / Talented leaper. / What am I? (The answer is: a whale.) As a class, create a collection of nouns, adjectives and verbs to describe the wildlife in the Southern Islands. Use this word bank to help pupils to create their own Kennings poems.

*   Ask pupils to write a leaflet about the Southern Islands, encouraging tourists to visit. Provide pupils with additional information on the Southern Islands from tourism websites which they can use alongside the information on pages 32 and 33 of the Study Book. They should include a description of the Southern Islands, the activities available and the wildlife that can be seen there. Encourage pupils to use pictures and plenty of descriptive and persuasive language to attract tourists.

*   The average temperature in South Georgia ranges from 4 °C in the summer to –5 °C in the winter, which is a range of 9 °C. Provide pupils with the information below and ask them to calculate the range in temperature. The figures show the average summer temperature followed by the average winter temperature: Argentina 25 °C / 12 °C. The Falkland Islands 10 °C / 2 °C. Venezuela 24 °C / 22 °C. Antarctica –60 °C / –28 °C. Ask pupils to compare these values to the UK (16 °C / 4 °C). Pupils could also plot the temperatures in a bar graph to visually compare the data.

World Zones 1

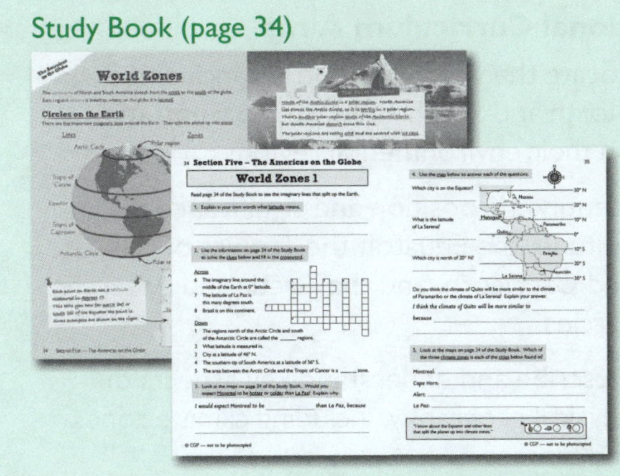

Study Book (page 34)

Activity Book (pages 34-35)

National Curriculum Aims

- Locate the world's countries, including North and South America, concentrating on their environmental regions.

- Identify the position and significance of latitude, the Equator, the Tropics of Cancer and Capricorn, and the Arctic and Antarctic Circles.

- Describe and understand key aspects of physical geography, including climate zones and biomes.

Introduction

This topic introduces pupils to the idea of latitude. The five major lines of latitude are: the Arctic Circle (66° N), the Tropic of Cancer (23° N), the Equator (0°), the Tropic of Capricorn (23° S) and the Antarctic Circle (66° S). The North Pole is located at 90° N, and the South Pole is at 90° S.

The Tropics were named around 2000 years ago, after the constellations of Capricorn (a goat) and Cancer (a crab). This is because at the time when the lines were named, the sun was positioned in the Capricorn constellation during the winter solstice and in the Cancer constellation during the summer solstice.

Answers to Activity Book Questions

1. How far north or south of the Equator somewhere in the world is.

2. Across: 6 — Equator, 7 — sixteen, 8 — South America
   Down: 1 — Polar, 2 — degrees, 3 — Montreal, 4 — Cape Horn, 5 — temperate

3. *I would expect Montreal to be* colder *than La Paz, because* it is further away from the Equator.

4. Quito — 30° S — Nassau
   E.g. *I think the climate of Quito will be more similar to* Paramaribo, *because* Quito is on the Equator and Paramaribo is close to the Equator/they have more similar latitudes and so they will have similar climates. La Serena is further away from the Equator.

5. *Montreal* — (north) temperate zone, *Cape Horn* — (south) temperate zone,
   Alert — (north) polar region, *La Paz* — The Tropics

Extra Activities

- Provide pupils with a world map, or globe, that includes latitude lines. Ask them to find the latitude of some major cities in North and South America (e.g. New York, Washington D.C., Vancouver, Mexico City, Rio de Janeiro). For each city, ask them to find another city on a different continent that has a similar latitude.

- To help pupils to understand latitude (and longitude), lay out a grid on the playground (or the floor of the sports hall), with 5 'latitude' lines and 5 'longitude' lines. Choose a location on the grid (e.g. latitude of 3, longitude of 4) and ask pupils to go to that location. Then choose several more locations, with pupils moving to that spot on the grid each time. This can then be transferred to using a sphere. Split pupils into groups and provide each group with a sphere (e.g. a ball) with lines of latitude and longitude marked on in different colours. Give pupils coordinates to find and ask them to give the colour of the two lines that meet there.

World Zones 2

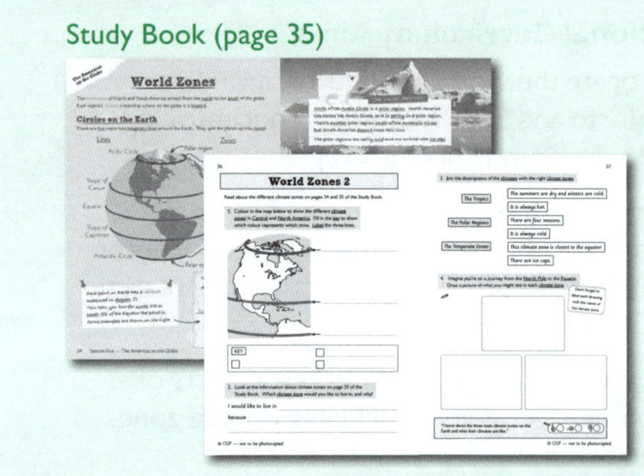

Study Book (page 35)

Activity Book (pages 36-37)

National Curriculum Aims

- Locate the world's countries, including North and South America, concentrating on their environmental regions.

- Identify the position and significance of latitude, the Equator, the Tropics of Cancer and Capricorn, and the Arctic and Antarctic Circles.

- Describe and understand key aspects of physical geography, including climate zones and biomes.

Introduction

Pupils can use this page to explore how the climate changes as the distance from the Equator increases. Latitude affects climate due to the amount of sunlight that reaches the Earth's surface. Energy from the sun hits the Earth most directly at the Equator. However, as latitude increases, energy from the sun strikes the Earth at lower angles, and the energy is spread out over a larger area. This could be demonstrated to pupils by darkening the classroom and shining a torch onto a globe.

We have seasons because of the tilt of the Earth's axis — when it is summer in the UK, the Northern Hemisphere is tilted towards the sun, so more energy reaches the UK and it is less spread out. When it's winter in the UK, the Northern Hemisphere is tilted away from the sun, so less energy reaches the UK.

Answers to Activity Book Questions

1. Any appropriate colouring-in that shows the polar region, temperate region and the Tropics.
    The lines (from top to bottom) are: Arctic Circle, Tropic of Cancer, Equator

2. Any appropriate answer, e.g. *I would like to live in* the Tropics, *because* I like hot weather and don't like winter.

3. The Tropics — It is always hot, This climate zone is closest to the Equator
    The Polar Regions — It is always cold, There are ice caps
    The Temperate Zones — The summers are dry and winters are cold, There are four seasons

4. E.g. pupils may draw a snow/ice covered scene for the polar region, an autumn scene for the temperate zone and a rainforest or savannah scene for the Tropics. They may also include appropriate plants and animals.

Extra Activities

- Split pupils into small groups and ask each group to use the internet to research the climate of one city near the Equator, such as Quito in Ecuador, Kampala in Uganda, and Pekanbaru in Indonesia. They could use the data they find to make graphs of rainfall and temperature to add to a wall display. As a class, discuss why the cities have different climates, despite all being close to the Equator (e.g. Quito is colder due to altitude).

- Show pupils pictures of nature illustrations by naturalists in the Americas and discuss why they were important for early naturalists (e.g. it allowed them to record what they saw so the same species could be easily identified by others, at a time before photography existed). This could include illustrations by Maria Merian, John James Audubon and Marianne North. Ask pupils to find a photo of a plant or animal in the Americas and create their own illustration in the style of one of the artists they have been shown.

- Ask pupils to each choose a climate zone or biome of the Americas (using pages 6, 7 and 35 of the Study Book) and to design an animal or plant to live in that area. Ask them to write a description of their creation, including the reason why their animal/plant would be well-suited to living in that climate zone/biome.

The Countries of Europe

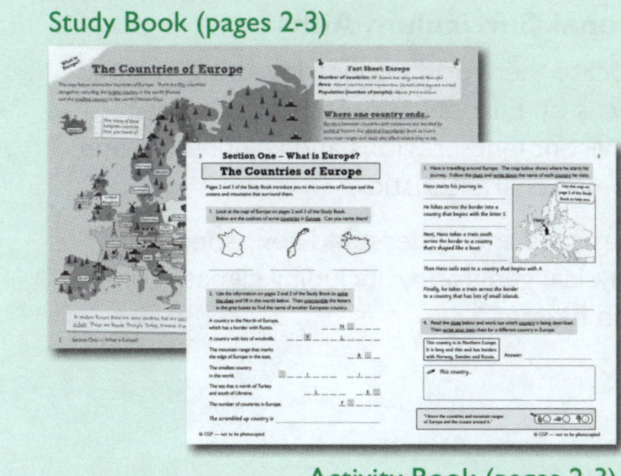

Study Book (pages 2-3)

Activity Book (pages 2-3)

National Curriculum Aims

- Locate the world's countries, using maps to focus on Europe, concentrating on key physical and human characteristics.

- Describe and understand key aspects of physical geography, including mountains.

- Use maps to locate and describe countries.

Introduction

Europe was formed when the supercontinent Pangaea broke up, which began around 200 million years ago. It first split into two continents, Laurasia and Gondwanaland. Laurasia then divided further into North America, Europe and Asia. Evidence for the existence of these supercontinents comes from several sources — the shapes of the continents indicate that they may have fitted together in the past (e.g. South America and Africa), there are shared rock types between continents, and there are similar fossils on different continents.

This topic introduces pupils to the countries that make up Europe. If pupils have been on holiday or have connections (e.g. relatives, pen-pals) in a European country, they could be encouraged to bring in photographs that could be displayed on a map of Europe in the classroom and referred to in subsequent lessons.

Answers to Activity Book Questions

1. France — Norway — Iceland

2. Finland — Netherlands — Ural — Vatican City — Black Sea — Fifty
    The scrambled up country is Latvia

3. Germany — Switzerland — Italy — Albania — Greece

4. *Answer:* Finland.
    For their own clues, pupils should use appropriate geographical vocabulary (e.g. east, west, north, south, border, sea etc.) to describe their chosen country accurately.

Extra Activities

- In groups or as a class, show pupils photographs of well-known landmarks from different countries in Europe (e.g. Eiffel Tower, Leaning Tower of Pisa, Sagrada Familia, Saint Basil's Cathedral in Moscow). Ask pupils to name the countries and cities that the landmarks are in and locate them on a map.

- Assign each pupil a different country in Europe and ask pupils to research the traditional food from the country, or a food that is grown in the country. The class could then have a 'foods of Europe' day where each pupil brings in the food that they found out about to share with the rest of the class.

- Show pupils pictures or animations of the supercontinent Pangaea, from which the current continents formed. Ask them to find the parts of Pangaea that broke apart to form Europe and see if they can identify any modern-day countries (e.g. on some diagrams of Pangaea, the Scandinavian countries are relatively easy to identify). Get pupils to label any countries they can identify.

Natural Europe 1

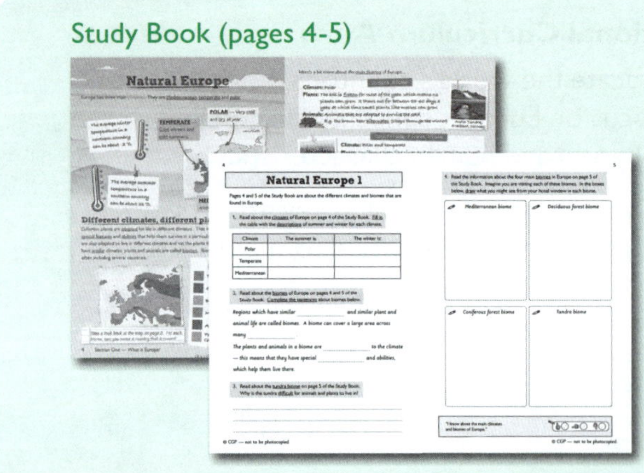

Study Book (pages 4-5)

Activity Book (pages 4-5)

National Curriculum Aims

- Locate the world's countries, using maps to focus on Europe, concentrating on their environmental regions and key physical and human characteristics.

- Describe and understand key aspects of physical geography, including climate zones and biomes.

Introduction

This topic focuses on the main climates and biomes that are found throughout Europe. Pupils might be interested to think about how the climate where they live compares to other countries. For example, the UK is colder and rainier than Mediterranean countries, but it is not the coldest or rainiest country in Europe. The country that receives the most rainfall annually is Montenegro. Kazakhstan and Russia are among the coldest countries, where winter temperatures can fall below −20 °C.

Answers to Activity Book Questions

1. Polar: *The summer is* cold and dry; *The winter is* cold and dry. Temperate: *The summer is* mild; *The winter is* cold. Mediterranean: *The summer is* hot and dry; *The winter is* mild.

2. *Regions which have similar* climates *and similar plant and animal life* are called biomes. *A biome can cover a large area across many* countries. *The plants and animals in a biome are* adapted *to the climate — this means that they have special* features *and abilities, which help them live there.*

3. E.g. it is very cold and the ground is frozen most of the year, so not many plants can grow and animals don't have much to eat.

4. Any appropriate drawings. The Mediterranean biome could include spiny plants. The deciduous forest biome should include deciduous trees, the coniferous forest biome should include conifers, and there should be few or no trees and large plants in the tundra biome. There could also be appropriate animals (e.g. bears in the tundra biome, porcupines in the Mediterranean biome).

Extra Activities

- Provide pupils with the average yearly rainfall, average June temperature and average December temperature for Rome, London and Oslo. Ask pupils to plot the data on bar charts and discuss in pairs whether the data matches what they would expect from a Mediterranean, temperate and polar climate.

- Split the class into four groups, and give each group a poster-sized piece of card with the name of one of the four main European biomes at the top. Get each group to make a collage representing that biome. They can cut out or draw pictures representing the weather, location, plant life and animal life in their biome and stick them to the poster. The posters could be used to make a class display about the biomes of Europe.

- Ask pupils to imagine that they are travel agents. Present them with a series of hypothetical customers with different needs and ask them to use the maps on pages 2-4 of the Study Book to select countries that would be appropriate. E.g. "Elijah wants to go somewhere hot with beaches to relax on and cities nearby to explore" (possible answers: Italy/Portugal). "Mohana loves nature and wants to go somewhere where she can see snowy mountains and large animals, like bears" (possible answers: Norway/Finland/Sweden).

Natural Europe 2

Study Book (pages 4-5)

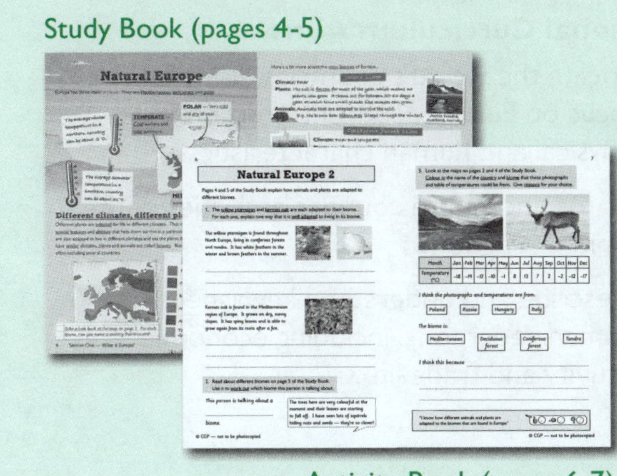

Activity Book (pages 6-7)

National Curriculum Aims

- Locate the world's countries, using maps to focus on Europe, concentrating on their environmental regions and key physical and human characteristics.

- Describe and understand key aspects of physical geography, including climate zones and biomes.

Introduction

The distribution of biomes in Europe is largely determined by the climate. This means that biomes are vulnerable to the effects of climate change. In Europe, climate change could change the distribution of the biomes, and the plant and animal species within them. For example, rising temperatures could lead to the melting of the permafrost in tundra biomes, which could allow coniferous forests to colonise those areas.

Answers to Activity Book Questions

1. Willow ptarmigan: E.g. having white feathers in the winter and brown in the summer means the willow ptarmigan is well camouflaged in both seasons and is less likely to be eaten.
    Kermes oak: E.g. there are lots of fires in the Mediterranean region, so being able to regrow after a fire means they can survive in that area.

2. *This person is talking about a* deciduous forest *biome.*

3. *Russia — Tundra*
    E.g. *I think this because* it is very cold in the winter and there are no trees in the photographs.

Extra Activities

- Provide pupils with pictures of animals/plants that live in Europe. Working in pairs, they should decide which biome each one lives in and why. Pupils could then choose one of the plants/animals and make a fact file about it, which could include its size, distribution and adaptations to the biome it's found in.

- Ask pupils to choose one of the biomes and find other places in the world where that biome occurs. They could research the climate, animals and plants of that area and use the information to explain why it is the same type of biome as the one they chose in Europe. They could then list any other similarities and differences between the two biomes.

- Show pupils videos and/or maps of the migration of birds between different parts of Europe. For example, pink-footed geese and brent geese breed in polar regions and migrate to the UK for the winter. In contrast, swallows that breed in the UK migrate south and overwinter in South Africa. Ask pupils why they think birds do this (to avoid cold winters and make sure they have enough food). They could also think about what adaptations birds need to be able to migrate long distances, such as being able to remember routes and navigate, and store enough energy to fly long distances.

Separated by Sea

Study Book (pages 6-7)

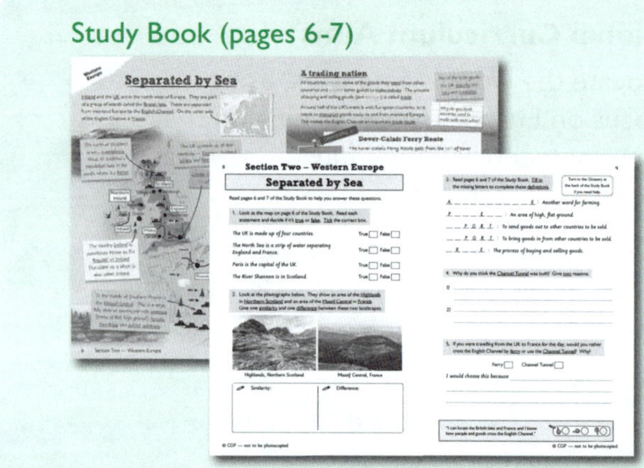

Activity Book (pages 8-9)

National Curriculum Aims

- Locate the world's countries, using maps to focus on Europe, concentrating on key physical and human characteristics.

- Name and locate counties and cities of the United Kingdom.

- Describe and understand key aspects of human geography, including economic activity and trade links.

Introduction

France is the largest country in Western Europe and over 80% of the land is covered by farmland and forests. The UK is also around 80% farmland and forest, but is some two and half times smaller than France. This topic also covers the transport of people and goods across the English Channel. After reading pages 6 and 7 of the Study Book, ask pupils if any of them have ever visited France. If so, how did they get there?

Answers to Activity Book Questions

1. True — False — False — False

2. E.g. *Similarity*: Both places have hills. *Difference*: There is a lot of flat land in the Massif Central. / There are more trees in the Massif Central. / The Highlands are rockier.

3. Agriculture, Plateau, Export, Import, Trade.

4. E.g. To make it easier to trade goods between the UK and mainland Europe. / To make it easier for people to travel from the UK to mainland Europe. / Because it's quicker than taking the ferry.

5. Pupils may choose either option. E.g. Channel Tunnel. *I would choose this because* it's faster than taking the ferry. / Ferry. *I would choose this because* I like boats and you'd be able to enjoy the scenery.

Extra Activities

- Ask pupils to pretend that they are MPs in the UK parliament in the 1980s discussing the possibility of building the Channel Tunnel. In groups, ask them to list as many pros and cons of building the tunnel as they can think of. E.g. Cons: expensive, harmful to the environment, danger of collapse or fires, possibility of people crossing illegally. Pros: easier trade with mainland Europe, job creation, less congestion on waterways, shorter journey time. (For lower ability pupils, you could provide them with a list of statements to sort into pros and cons.) Once pupils have made their lists, they can debate the issue and vote on whether or not the tunnel should be built.

- As a class, make a list of foods that are grown in the UK, and therefore could be exported. Then make a list of foods pupils think are imported from abroad. Provide the class with packaging from foods bought in supermarkets, or ask pupils to bring some in. Pupils can check the country of origin on the packaging to see if it was imported and from where.

- Cut squares of card of different sizes to represent the approximate areas of the countries listed below. In groups, ask pupils to guess which square of card represents which country, then reveal the correct answers to the class. Ask pupils if they are surprised by the difference in size of the countries. (The areas are: Monaco — 1.5 cm x 1.5 cm, Northern Ireland — 3.5 cm x 3.5 cm, Wales — 4.5 cm x 4.5 cm, Republic of Ireland — 8 cm x 8 cm, Scotland — 9 cm x 9 cm, England — 11.5 cm x 11.5 cm, France — 25.5 cm x 25.5 cm.)

The Centre of the Union

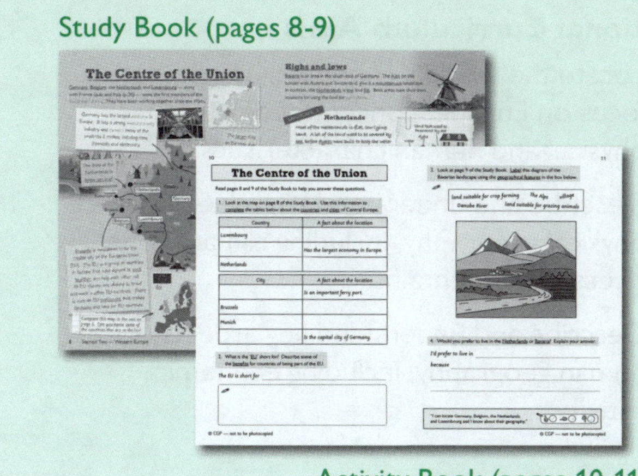

Study Book (pages 8-9)

Activity Book (pages 10-11)

National Curriculum Aims

- Locate the world's countries, using maps to focus on Europe, concentrating on key physical and human characteristics.

- Describe and understand key aspects of human geography, including land use, economic activity, trade links and the distribution of natural resources (including food).

Introduction

This topic introduces pupils to four of the original six member countries of the European Union. In 1944, Belgium, the Netherlands and Luxembourg formed one of the first trade unions, known as the Benelux Union, to facilitate trade between these three countries. It was this union that would form the foundation for the EU.

Answers to Activity Book Questions

1. Table 1: *Luxembourg* — e.g. The capital of Luxembourg is Luxembourg City. Germany — *Has the largest economy in Europe.* Netherlands — e.g. A third of the Netherlands is below sea level. Table 2: Rotterdam — *Is an important ferry port.* Brussels — e.g. Brussels is the capital city of the EU. *Munich* — e.g. Munich is south of the River Danube. Berlin — *Is the capital city of Germany.*

2. *The EU is short for* the European Union. E.g. Citizens of EU countries can travel and work in other EU countries. EU countries work together and help each other out.

3. Pupils should have labelled the river, mountains and village with the appropriate labels. Their labels should also distinguish between crop farming on the flat land by the river and grazing animals on the hilly land.

4. Pupils may answer either way, as long as they give sensible reasons for their choice. E.g. *I'd prefer to live in* Bavaria *because* there are mountains and I'd like to go mountain climbing. / *I'd prefer to live in* the Netherlands *because* there is a lot of farmland and flowers and I think it would be really pretty.

Extra Activities

- Give pupils an outline map of Europe without the country names marked on. Tell them that the first member countries of the group that became the EU were Belgium, Germany, France, Italy, Luxembourg and the Netherlands. Ask them to shade those countries in one colour. Then provide them with a list of the countries that subsequently joined and the year they joined. Get pupils to shade in the countries in different colours depending on the year they joined, and create a key to indicate which colour signifies which year. 1973 — UK, Ireland, Denmark, 1981 — Greece, 1986 — Spain, Portugal, 1995 — Austria, Finland, Sweden, 2004 — Cyprus, the Czech Republic, Estonia, Hungary, Latvia, Lithuania, Malta, Poland, Slovakia, Slovenia, 2007 — Bulgaria, Romania, 2013 — Croatia.

- Show pupils a picture of the highest mountain in Bavaria (the Zugspitze) and the lowest point in the Netherlands (the Zuidplaspolder). Tell them that a land mass has to be 600 metres or more above sea level to be classed as a mountain and that Mount Everest is 8848 metres above sea level. Pupils take it in turns to guess the height of the Zugspitze while you say 'higher or lower' to direct them to the correct answer of 2962 metres. Help them to understand how high this is by working out approximately how this compares with the altitude of their school. Repeat the activity to get pupils to work out the maximum depth of the Zuidplaspolder, which is −6.8 metres (6.8 metres below sea level).

The Iberian Peninsula

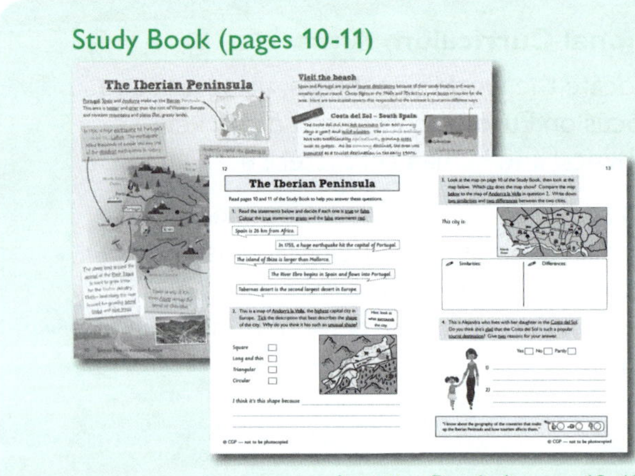

Study Book (pages 10-11)

Activity Book (pages 12-13)

National Curriculum Aims

- Locate the world's countries, using maps to focus on Europe, concentrating on key physical and human characteristics.

- Describe and understand key aspects of physical geography, including climate zones, rivers and mountains.

- Describe and understand key aspects of human geography, including economic activity.

Introduction

This topic introduces pupils to the three countries that make up the Iberian Peninsula. The name comes from the Greek for the River Ebro — Iberus. The peninsula is separated from the rest of Europe by the Pyrenees.

Answers to Activity Book Questions

1. False — True — False — False — False

2. Pupils should have ticked *long and thin*. E.g. *I think it's this shape because* there are mountains around it. / It's between mountains. / It's in a valley.

3. *This city is* Porto. *Similarities:* e.g. both cities have shops/museums/restaurants/hotels. / Both cities have a river flowing through them. *Differences:* e.g. There are no mountains around Porto. / Porto is by the sea and Andorra la Vella isn't.

4. Any appropriate answer. Pupils should draw on information from the Study Book. E.g. Partly. Tourism brings a lot of money to the area and creates jobs. / Tourism makes the cost of living very high for locals. / Building large resorts harms wildlife and can cause the coastline to wear away.

Extra Activities

- Tell pupils that the 1755 earthquake in Lisbon, Portugal was one of the most destructive recorded in human history. (Seismologists today estimate the magnitude was in the region of 8.5–9.0). Its epicentre was about 200 km away in the Atlantic Ocean. Show pupils a video about the earthquake and the resulting tsunami and firestorm. Ask pupils to imagine that they are a person living in Lisbon at the time of the earthquake and to write a diary entry from that person's point of view. What did they witness? How did they feel during and after the event? What will they do now that the city is almost totally destroyed?

- Get pupils to research the Tabernas Desert in Spain. As a class, discuss the key features of a desert (e.g. salty soil, low rainfall, high temperatures). Search online for a short video about deserts to show the class. In small groups, get pupils to plan what they would need to take on a two-day trek through the desert. List some factors for them to consider, e.g. shelter, food, water, protection from the cold/heat, entertainment. They could describe their plan in a presentation to the rest of the class or in written form. Alternatively, provide pupils with an outline of a suitcase and ask them to draw and label the items they would pack.

- Give pupils a selection of travel magazines trying to attract people to Spain, Portugal or Andorra. Alternatively, if any pupils have been on holiday to one of these countries, they could describe their experience to their classmates. Ask pupils to imagine that they have been on holiday to a place in one of these countries and use the information from the brochures and/or their classmates' descriptions to write a short story about what they did, saw and ate.

Scandinavia

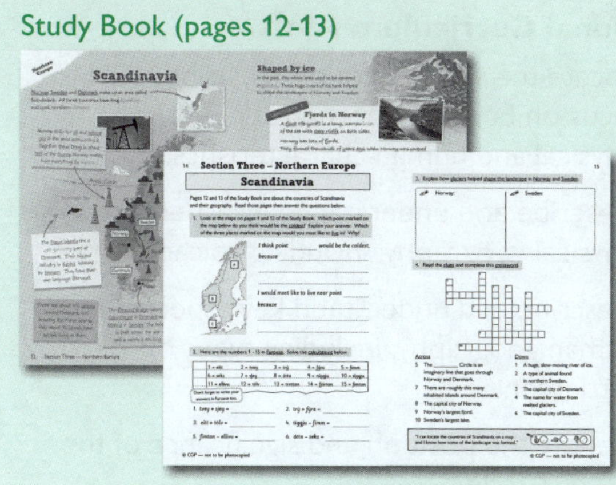

Study Book (pages 12-13)

Activity Book (pages 14-15)

National Curriculum Aims

- Locate the world's countries, using maps to focus on Europe, concentrating on key physical and human characteristics.

- Describe and understand key aspects of physical geography, including climate zones.

- Describe and understand key aspects of human geography, including economic activity and the distribution of natural resources.

Introduction

This topic introduces pupils to the countries of Scandinavia. Norway, Sweden and Denmark are famous for their Viking history, but today they are also well-known for having some of the highest standards of living in the world, and for being home to many noted inventors. Many everyday items such as the zip, aerosol cans and LEGO® were invented by Scandinavians.

Answers to Activity Book Questions

1. E.g. *I think point* A *would be the coldest, because* it's furthest north / it's closer to the North Pole. *I would most like to live near point* C *because* it would be the warmest and I don't like really cold weather.

2. 1. níggju (2 + 7 = 9) 2. sjey (3 + 4 = 7) 3. trettan (1 + 12 = 13)
    4. fimm (10 − 5 = 5) 5. fýra (15 − 11 = 4) 6. tvey (8 − 6 = 2)

3. E.g. *Norway*: Glaciers created the fjords by carving deep, narrow valleys into the land. When the glaciers melted, the valleys were flooded by the sea.
    Sweden: Glaciers created many lakes by carving hollows into the land which were filled with water from the glaciers when they melted.

4. Across: 5 Arctic, 7 seventy, 8 Oslo, 9 Sognefjord, 10 Vänern
    Down: 1 glacier, 2 bear, 3 Copenhagen, 4 meltwater, 6 Stockholm

Extra Activities

- Ask pupils to compare a city in Norway or Sweden with a city in southern Europe, such as Seville. They should compare average temperatures, average snowfall, and average days of sunshine. Their findings can be given in numerical form alongside a written explanation.

- Get pupils to investigate how slowly glaciers move. The Jostedal Glacier in Norway can move up to 100 cm per day. Ask pupils to calculate how far the glacier travels in 1 hour. They can then work out how far the glacier would move during the space of a lesson or the whole school day. They could mark the glacier's 'progress' on the floor with chalk throughout the day.

- Introduce pupils to some of the key features of Scandinavia's Viking heritage, particularly the Viking traditions of shipbuilding and sailing. Ask pupils why they think the Vikings became so good at seafaring (sailing was important to them for trade, travel and fishing). Search online for a map showing the expansion of the Vikings across Europe. What do pupils notice about the areas where the Vikings settled? Pupils can compare this map to the map of Europe on page 2 of the Study Book to work out the names of the countries the Vikings sailed to.

Land of the Midnight Sun

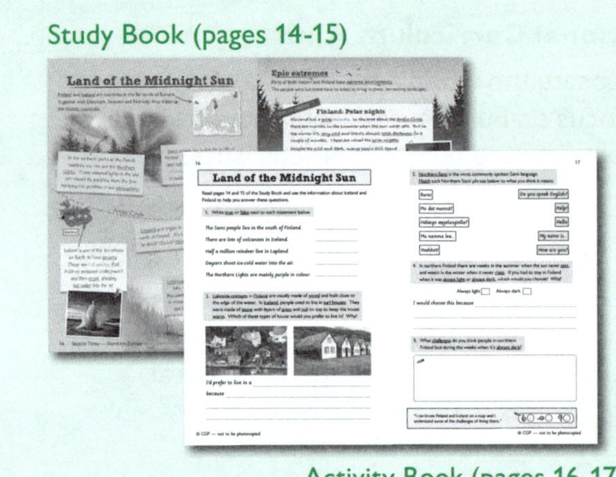

Study Book (pages 14-15)

Activity Book (pages 16-17)

National Curriculum Aims

- Locate the world's countries, using maps to focus on Europe, concentrating on key physical and human characteristics.

- Describe and understand key aspects of physical geography, including volcanoes.

- Describe and understand key aspects of human geography, including types of settlement.

- Identify the position and significance of the Arctic Circle.

Introduction

In Finland and Iceland, the best time to see the Northern Lights (*aurora borealis*) is in winter. The lights are caused by charged particles from the Sun (protons and electrons) colliding with gas particles in the Earth's atmosphere (e.g. oxygen and nitrogen). The collisions result in light being emitted — the colour of the light depends on the gas and the amount of energy involved in the collision. This phenomenon also occurs in the southern polar regions, where it's known as the *aurora australis*.

Answers to Activity Book Questions

1. False — True — False — False — False

2. Any appropriate answer. Pupils can draw on information from the Study Book and the photos provided. E.g. *I'd prefer to live in a* lakeside cottage *because* I could go swimming in the lake every day. / *I'd prefer to live in a* turf house *because* I want to live in Iceland and the grass and soil would keep the house warm.

3. Bures — Hello, Mo dat manná? — How are you?, Hálatgo Eaŋgelasgiella? — Do you speak English?, Mu namma lea... — My name is..., Veahket! — Help!

4. Pupils may answer either way, as long as they give sensible reasons for their answer. E.g. Always light. *I would choose this because* then I could always see what I was doing and could spend lots of time outside.

5. E.g. People can't see where they're going without a torch/electricity / can't generate solar energy / people could feel unhappy without sunlight/may not have enough vitamin D.

Extra Activities

- Show pupils pictures and a video about the Northern Lights. Then read them the extract from the end of Philip Pullman's 'Northern Lights' where Lyra first sees into a parallel universe. Ask them to look at a picture of the real Northern Lights and write a description of an invented town, city or seaside resort which they could imagine glimpsing amongst the strange colours.

- Ask pupils to create pictures to represent a polar night, using black paper and coloured pastels or paints. Underneath, they could write a haiku such as: The sunshine has gone / Yet we remain together / Safe under the stars.

- Search online for a short video about geysers to show to the class. Working in small groups outside, pupils can replicate the action of a geyser by dropping around seven Mentos® into a large bottle of diet cola and observing the eruption that follows. Explain to pupils that the sweets cause the cola to release gas bubbles, which quickly build up pressure, causing the cola to erupt from the top of the bottle in the same way that bubbles from boiling water underground cause pressure to build until a geyser erupts.

The Baltic Nations

Study Book (pages 16-17)

National Curriculum Aims

- Locate the world's countries, using maps to focus on Europe, concentrating on key physical and human characteristics.

- Describe and understand key aspects of human geography, including land use, economic activity, trade links and the distribution of natural resources (including energy).

Activity Book (pages 18-19)

Introduction

The Baltic Nations had a troubled history through the majority of the 20th century. Having established themselves as independent states in the early 1900s, in 1940 they were illegally incorporated into the Soviet Union. Then in 1941, German forces invaded the region. The Soviet Union reclaimed the Baltic Nations in 1944, and they remained part of the USSR for several decades. In the latter years of Soviet occupation, many protests took place in these countries, notably the Baltic Way, which saw 2 million people join hands to create a human chain of over 670 km. The chain stretched from Tallinn, through Riga to Vilnius. The Baltic Nations finally achieved independence in 1991.

Answers to Activity Book Questions

1. The Pärnu is a river in this country. — Estonia. Over half of this country is covered by forests. — Latvia. An important port in Lithuania. — Klaipėda. The capital of Lithuania. — Vilnius.

2. *Unlike some other countries, Lithuania doesn't have a lot of* fossil fuel *resources. Lithuania* imports *a lot of its energy from other countries with more resources. But it is starting to produce more* renewable energy. *This means using natural resources like water and* wind *to generate energy, or using plants and animal waste to make* biofuels.

3. Any appropriate answer outlining the pros and cons of oil shale. Pupils should draw on information from the Study Book. E.g. Lisandra: We use oil shale to produce electricity which we need. There's so much of it under Estonia, why wouldn't we use it? Mattias: We should be using greener energy sources like wind power and solar power, because burning oil shale is really bad for the environment.

4. Across: 1 Venta, 5 Tallinn, 6 computer, 8 freezes   Down: 2 twenty, 3 Union, 4 biofuels, 7 rock, 9 Riga

Extra Activities

- Provide pupils with the data below which details the percentage of electricity that comes from each energy source in Lithuania and the UK. Lithuania — fossil fuels: 73%, nuclear fuels: 0%, hydroelectricity: 4%, wind: 12%, other renewables (including tidal, solar and geothermal): 11%. UK — fossil fuels: 50%, nuclear fuels: 9%, hydroelectricity: 2%, wind: 15% other renewables: 24%. Ask pupils to make a bar chart or pie charts to compare the two countries. They could also write two or three sentences under their charts, stating some similarities and differences between energy production in the UK and Lithuania.

- Search online for a time-lapse map of Europe over the last thousand years and show pupils how the countries have changed. Ask pupils to watch out for changes around the time of WW2, increases and decreases in the number of countries, and the emergence of the Baltic Nations. Also ask them to note what happens to England, France and Spain over the last thousand years (their borders don't change much) and suggest some reasons why this might be (i.e. physical barriers such as seas/mountains). Discuss some of the reasons why countries change their borders (e.g. wars, invasions, rebellions, empires).

Land of the Alps

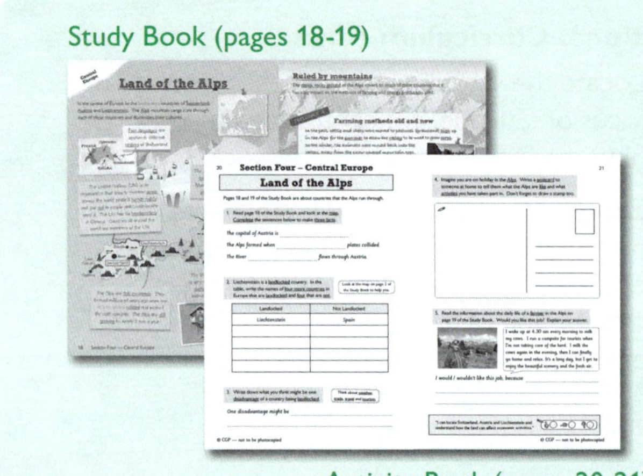

Study Book (pages 18-19)

Activity Book (pages 20-21)

National Curriculum Aims

- Locate the world's countries, using maps to focus on Europe, concentrating on key physical and human characteristics.

- Describe and understand key aspects of physical geography, including climate zones.

- Describe and understand key aspects of human geography, including types of land use and the distribution of energy resources.

Introduction

As an introduction to this topic, you could read pupils parts of the first chapter of 'Heidi' by Johanna Spyri, which describes Heidi's first journey into the Alps. In it, there are descriptions of different geographical areas of the mountain range. Then ask pupils to use what they've heard to describe what they think it might be like to live in the Alps.

Answers to Activity Book Questions

1. *The capital of Austria is* Vienna. *The Alps formed when* tectonic *plates collided.*
    The River Danube *flows through Austria.*

2. Any appropriate answers.

3. E.g. *One disadvantage might be* that trade with other countries is more difficult because it's harder to ship things by sea.

4. Any appropriate answer. Pupils should draw on information from pages 18 and 19 of the Study Book.

5. Any appropriate answer. Pupils should draw on the information provided in the question and on page 19 of the Study Book. E.g. *I would* like this job, because I'd get to be outside all the time and enjoy the views.

Extra Activities

- Choose a location described in the first chapter of 'Heidi', such as Grandfather's cottage. Alternatively, read the description of the mountain in the third chapter of the book to the class. Ask pupils to use the description to draw a picture showing how they imagine the location to look.

- Remind pupils that the United Nations has its headquarters in Geneva. Ask pupils to read about the aims of the UN on page 18 of the Study Book. Then ask them to debate an issue, for example whether police officers should carry guns, or whether a country should only give financial aid to its own people.

- Demonstrate to the class how fold mountains form. Create a stack of towels (each towel should be folded in half lengthways) and place a box on either end of the pile. Tell two pupils to push the boxes together slowly until the towels fold up, resembling mountains. Explain to pupils that the towels represent the layers of rock that make up the Earth's crust and that the boxes represent two tectonic plates. Tell pupils that fold mountains only occur near plate boundaries. The Alps were formed by this geological process between 30 and 40 million years ago. Other fold mountains include the Himalayas, Andes and Appalachians — provide pupils with a map or globe and ask them to mark the locations of these mountain ranges.

In the Middle

Study Book (pages 20-21)

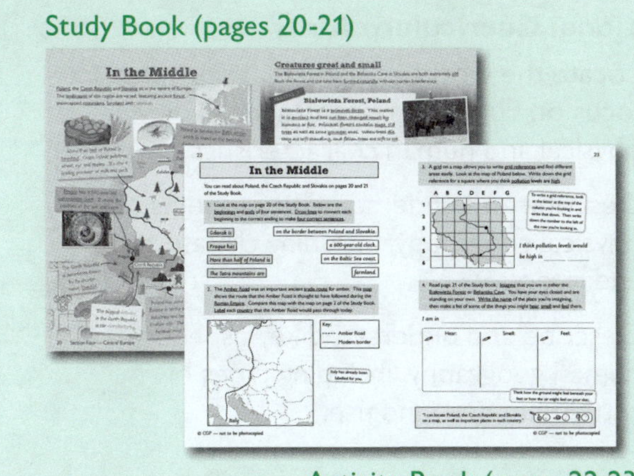

Activity Book (pages 22-23)

National Curriculum Aims

* Locate the world's countries, using maps to focus on Europe, concentrating on their environmental regions, key physical and human characteristics, and major cities.

* Understand geographical similarities and differences by studying the human geography of a region in a European country.

* Describe and understand key aspects of human geography, including types of settlement and land use.

Introduction

The Czech Republic and Slovakia have existed as two independent countries only since the early 1990s. Until then (since 1918), they had existed as a single country (Czechoslovakia). They are both members of the Visegrád Group, or the Visegrád Four. This group also contains Poland and Hungary and was set up to allow the four countries to cooperate closely with one another. In 2016, the Czech Republic officially adopted the shorter name, Czechia, in the same way that France is the official short name for the French Republic.

Answers to Activity Book Questions

1. Gdansk is — on the Baltic Sea coast. Prague has — a 600-year-old clock. More than half of Poland is — farmland. The Tatra mountains are — on the border between Poland and Slovakia.

2. Pupils should have labelled Poland, the Czech Republic, Slovakia, Austria, Hungary and Slovenia. They may also have labelled Russia.

3. Pupils should identify that pollution levels will be high near cities. E.g. E5 / C1 / E3.

4. Any appropriate answer. Pupils should draw on information from page 21 of the Study Book. E.g. *I am in* Białowieża Forest. *Hear*: leaves rustling in the wind, insects buzzing, bison walking around, a wolf howling. *Smell*: rotting trees, fresh air. *Feel*: leaves and dead plants under my feet. It's not too hot because I'm in the shade.

Extra Activities

* Show pupils a video about how stalactites and stalagmites grow and how they can sometimes join together to make columns. After looking at pictures of the Belianska Cave, ask pupils to make their own versions of stalactites and stalagmites using papier mâché and paint, or modelling clay.

* As a class, list reasons for air pollution. Look at the list and ask pupils what they think that cities can do to reduce air pollution. Following this, pupils can make their own pollutant catcher to study the air quality in their area. They will need a paper plate, string and petroleum jelly. Pupils will need to make two holes 10 cm apart along the edge of the plate and thread some string through so that the plate can be hung vertically. Spread the petroleum jelly on the front of the plate. Hang the plate in a sheltered location outside for up to two weeks. If black dots appear on the petroleum jelly, this indicates that there may be pollutants in the air.

* Split the class into two groups. Provide each group with a large sheet of paper and a marker pen. Get the first group to use books or online resources to list as many species of birds that live in the Białowieża Forest as they can. Ask the second group to do the same for an ancient woodland in the UK (such as Sherwood Forest or Epping Forest). Pupils can then compare and contrast their lists as a class.

Following the Danube

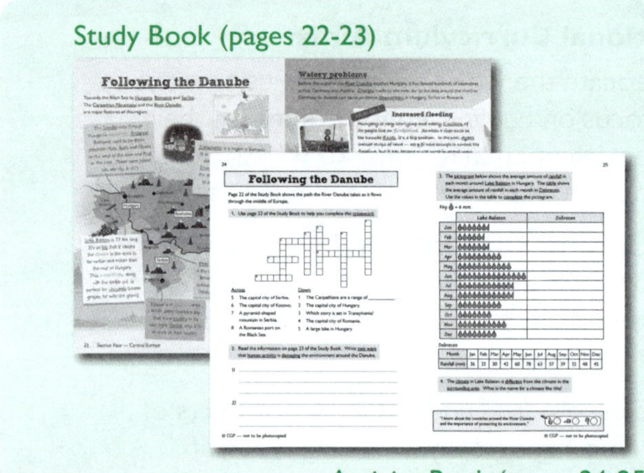

Study Book (pages 22-23)

Activity Book (pages 24-25)

National Curriculum Aims

- Locate the world's countries, using maps to focus on Europe, concentrating on key physical and human characteristics.

- Describe and understand key aspects of physical geography, including climate zones and rivers.

- Describe and understand key aspects of human geography, including types of settlement and land use.

Introduction

The River Danube is the second longest river in Europe. It is approximately 2900 km long and passes through 10 countries — Germany, Austria, Slovakia, Hungary, Croatia, Serbia, Bulgaria, Romania, Moldova, and Ukraine. It has been integral in shaping the political landscape of central Europe and has often served as a boundary between empires. For example, for a long time, the Danube acted as part of the border of the Roman Empire.

Answers to Activity Book Questions

1. Across: 5 Belgrade, 6 Prishtina, 7 Rtanj, 8 Sulina
    Down: 1 mountains, 2 Budapest, 3 Dracula, 4 Bucharest, 5 Balaton

2. E.g. building on floodplains means that more rainwater flows back into the river and causes flooding. Building dams across the river traps sediment and stops it reaching the Danube Delta, resulting in parts of it eroding away.

3. Pupils should have correctly recorded the values provided in the table as a pictogram using symbols that match the key, as shown on the right.

4. Microclimate.

	Debrecen
Jan	🌢🌢🌢🌢🌢🌢
Feb	🌢🌢🌢🌢🌢
Mar	🌢🌢🌢🌢🌢
Apr	🌢🌢🌢🌢🌢🌢
May	🌢🌢🌢🌢🌢🌢🌢🌢
Jun	🌢🌢🌢🌢🌢🌢🌢🌢🌢🌢🌢
Jul	🌢🌢🌢🌢🌢🌢🌢🌢🌢🌢
Aug	🌢🌢🌢🌢🌢🌢🌢🌢
Sep	🌢🌢🌢🌢🌢🌢
Oct	🌢🌢🌢🌢🌢🌢
Nov	🌢🌢🌢🌢🌢🌢🌢
Dec	🌢🌢🌢🌢🌢🌢🌢

Extra Activities

- Page 23 of the Study Book talks about how building on floodplains upstream can increase the risk of flooding downstream. Demonstrate with a bucket of water or a hosepipe how bare earth soaks up excess water, whilst water stays on top of concrete. Get pupils to carry out their own investigations into which surfaces are the most and least absorbent by pouring water onto a range of natural and man-made surfaces and recording their findings.

- Tell pupils that the Danube Delta is the largest wetland in Europe and explain how human activity is putting the environment under pressure. Divide the class into groups and ask each one to research a different river delta, such as the Mississippi Delta (USA), the Nile Delta (Egypt), the Mekong Delta (Vietnam) and the Ganges Delta (India and Bangladesh). Ask pupils to look at how the deltas are being affected by human activity, the wildlife and plant life under threat, how the local human population is suffering, e.g. because of flooding, and what steps are being taken to protect the deltas. Each group could then do a presentation to report their findings to the rest of the class.

- Split pupils into small groups and give each group a photo of a point of interest along the River Danube (e.g. the centre of Budapest, the centre of Belgrade, Esztergom Basilica, Iron Gates gorge, Golubac Fortress, the Danube Delta, the Danube Bridge between Giurgui and Ruse, the Danube Bend near Visegrád). Ask pupils to create artworks inspired by these places, and use them to make a class display of the sights along the Danube.

Crossing Into Asia

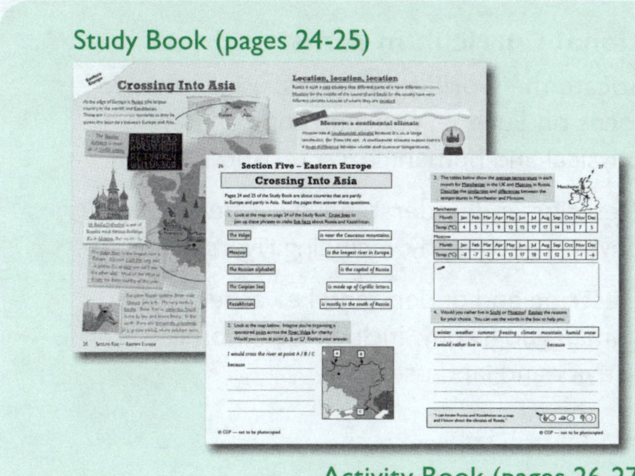

Study Book (pages 24-25)

Activity Book (pages 26-27)

National Curriculum Aims

- Locate the world's countries, using maps to focus on Europe (including Russia), concentrating on key physical and human characteristics.

- Describe and understand key aspects of physical geography, including climate zones, biomes, rivers and mountains.

Introduction

This topic covers Russia and Kazakhstan, which straddle the border of Asia and Europe.

Answers to Activity Book Questions

1. The Volga — is the longest river in Europe. Moscow — is the capital of Russia. The Russian alphabet — is made up of Cyrillic letters. The Caspian Sea — is near the Caucasus mountains. Kazakhstan — is mostly to the south of Russia.

2. Pupils may choose any location, as long as they give sensible reasons for their choice. E.g. *I would cross the river at point* C *because* it's further south so it would be warmer.

3. E.g. It's warmer in Manchester than Moscow in winter. Manchester and Moscow are roughly the same temperature in summer.

4. E.g. I would rather live in Moscow because it has a continental *climate* which means the *weather* is *freezing* and snowy in *winter*. I could play in the *snow* in winter, but there would still be nice weather in the *summer*.

Extra Activities

- Ask pupils why some countries are bigger than others. E.g. why is Russia bigger than the UK? Key words to use in their discussions are: natural borders (seas, mountains, forests), wars, empires. Get pupils to look at a map of the world and try to work out the top ten largest countries, with Russia in first place. They can check their answers by using an atlas or online resources to find out the size of each country in square kilometres. They could present this data in the form of a table or graph.

- The ten longest rivers in Europe are the Volga, Danube, Ural, Dnieper, Don, Pechora, Kama, Kura, Oka and Belaya. Split the class into pairs or groups of three and give each group a river to research. Ask each group to create a fact file on their river (using books and/or online resources). Their fact file should include the river's course plotted on a map of Europe, its length, and the names of the countries it passes through.

- Tell pupils the Russian folk tale of 'Babushka'. In the folk tale, Babushka refuses to accompany the three kings when they visit the baby Jesus, saying she has too much housework to do. Later she regrets her decision and sets off to find them, delivering presents to children as she goes. The story is the Russian version of Santa Claus, with Babushka continuing her journey to this day. After reading the story, ask pupils to map out a journey Babushka could take across Russia. Remind them that Russia has three main biomes as well as a variety of natural features, human settlements and nature which should factor into their plan. Pupils should use the information in the Study Book to write a short story or produce a comic strip about the journey. Elements of the story could include her traversing particular rivers, climbing certain mountains and conversing with different animals and people.

The Eastern Edge

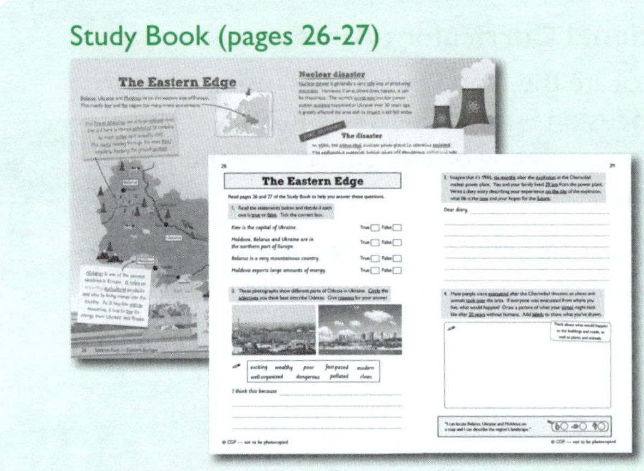

Study Book (pages 26-27)

Activity Book (pages 28-29)

National Curriculum Aims

- Locate the world's countries, using maps to focus on Europe, concentrating on key physical and human characteristics.

- Describe and understand key aspects of physical geography, including rivers.

- Describe and understand key aspects of human geography, including economic activity and land use.

Introduction

Belarus, Ukraine and Moldova have strong historical ties to Russia and only became independent republics in 1991, following the collapse of the Soviet Union. All three of these countries are amongst the top ten poorest countries in Europe, largely as a result of the economic upheaval following the dissolution of the Soviet Union.

Ukraine is the largest European country to be entirely located within the continent. A huge 71% of Ukraine's land is used for farming and over 80% of that is used for crops. Grain production makes up a significant part of the economy — Ukraine is the 9th largest wheat producer in the world and the 6th largest producer of corn.

Answers to Activity Book Questions

1. True — False — False — False

2. Pupils may circle any adjectives as long as they give sensible reasons for their answer. E.g. Wealthy/modern. *I think this because* there are tall, modern-looking skyscrapers.

3. Any appropriate answer. Pupils may include a description of the explosion, their subsequent evacuation and the fact that they have not been allowed to return home. Their hopes for the future could include being able to go home or that they or their family won't become ill from the effects of the radiation.

4. Any appropriate answer specific to the place where each pupil lives. Pupils should show abandoned buildings and roads becoming run down, animals like cats, foxes and badgers taking over the area, and plants and trees growing everywhere.

Extra Activities

- Find a video online about nuclear power to show the class. Ask half the class to write speeches in favour of using nuclear power, and the other half to write speeches arguing against it. Hold a class debate about whether the UK government should continue to allow the building of nuclear power stations in this country.

- Tell the pupils that despite the risk of radiation, approximately 150 people never left the area around Chernobyl and that some people are keen to move there. Ask the pupils why they think that might be. Some reasons include people not wanting to leave their homes, fighting elsewhere (e.g. due to Russia's involvement in Crimea), the cheapness of land and housing, and the peace and quiet of the area.

- Ukraine has many flat plains of chernozem, which is a very fertile soil. Divide the pupils into groups of three and give each pupil a small pot. Tell the groups to collect three different soil samples from the school grounds. Ask them to write a description of their soil type in terms of: colour (black, dark brown, light brown, etc.), amount of humus (does it feel moist and crumbly?), smoothness (is it clay-like?) and sandiness (does it feel rough, grainy and uneven?). Ask pupils to predict which soil would be best for growing crops, then give each pupil some cress seeds to allow them to test their hypothesis.

At the Ends of Europe

Study Book (pages 28-29)

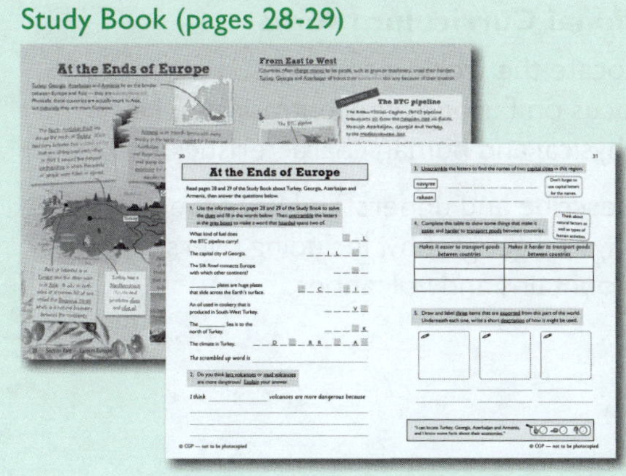

Activity Book (pages 30-31)

National Curriculum Aims

- Locate the world's countries, using maps to focus on Europe, concentrating on key physical and human characteristics.

- Describe and understand key aspects of physical geography, including rivers.

- Describe and understand key aspects of human geography, including economic activity, trade links and land use.

Introduction

Turkey, Georgia, Azerbaijan and Armenia, along with Russia and Kazakhstan, lie across the boundary of Europe and Asia. Georgia, Azerbaijan and Armenia (as well as southern Russia) are part of the Caucasus region, which lies between the Black Sea and Caspian Sea and includes the Caucasus mountains. The region is culturally and linguistically diverse, with more than 30 languages spoken there.

Answers to Activity Book Questions

1. <u>O</u>il, <u>T</u>bili<u>s</u>i, A<u>s</u>ia, <u>t</u>ec<u>t</u>onic, oliv<u>e</u>, Bla<u>c</u>k, Me<u>d</u>it<u>e</u>rra<u>n</u>ean. *The scrambled up word is* continents.

2. Pupils may answer either way, as long as they give a sensible reason for their answer. E.g. *I think* lava *volcanoes are more dangerous, because* lava is very hot and it would burn everything it touched.

3. Yerevan — Ankara

4. Easier: e.g. roads / ports / countries being friendly/working together
    Harder: e.g. mountain ranges / wars / closed borders / rivers / seas/oceans between countries

5. E.g. Olive oil (for cooking), grains/wheat (for food/making bread), oil (for fuel).

Extra Activities

- Briefly introduce the class to plate tectonics or recap what they already know. Explain to them that the Earth's surface is split into plates, and that volcanoes and earthquakes are more likely to occur where plates meet. Provide pupils with a blank map of the world and ask them to colour in the Eurasian plate and, using an atlas, label the countries which they think are most at risk from natural disasters related to tectonic plates. Pupils can check their predictions by searching online for earthquakes or volcanic eruptions in those countries.

- Show pupils pictures or videos of mud volcanoes. Divide pupils into small groups and ask them to build their own mud volcano model. Method: 1) Take an empty plastic bottle and place scrunched-up newspaper around it in a rough cone shape. 2) Use masking tape to keep the newspaper in place and cover with papier mâché. 3) Paint grey and use a waterproof varnish. 4) Add 4 tsp of bicarbonate of soda and 150 ml of warm water mixed with grey food colouring to the bottle. 5) Add 60 ml of vinegar to make the volcano erupt.

- Discuss the information about the Silk Road in the Study Book. Ask pupils to list the pros and cons of ancient people choosing to travel that route, e.g. illness, danger, accumulation of wealth, experiencing different cultures and meeting new people. Show the class some illustrations of ancient travellers on the Silk Road (available online). Ask pupils to write an account of a journey from Europe into Asia and back.

Around the Adriatic

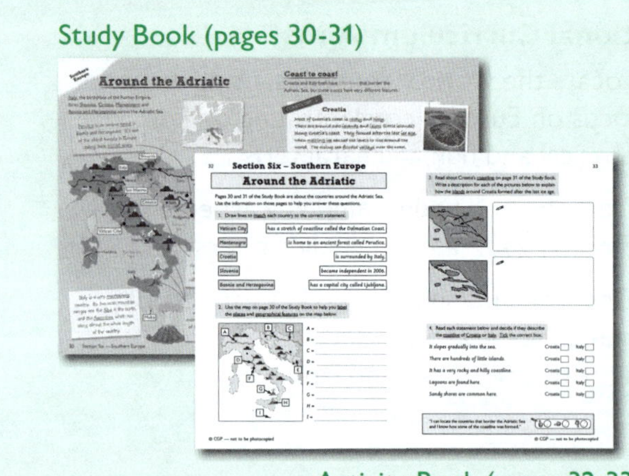

Study Book (pages 30-31)

Activity Book (pages 32-33)

National Curriculum Aims

- Locate the world's countries, using maps to focus on Europe, concentrating on key physical and human characteristics.

- Describe and understand key aspects of physical geography, including rivers, mountains and volcanoes.

Introduction

This topic introduces pupils to the countries that border the Adriatic Sea. This area was once a central part of the Roman Empire and many archaeological sites still remain, from the Colosseum and the Pantheon in Rome to Diocletian's Palace in Split, Croatia.

Answers to Activity Book Questions

1. Vatican City — is surrounded by Italy. Montenegro — became independent in 2006.
    Croatia — has a stretch of coastline called the Dalmatian Coast. Slovenia — has a capital city called
    Ljubljana. Bosnia and Herzegovina — is home to an ancient forest called Perućica.

2. A = Milan, B = Zagreb, C = River Sava, D = River Tiber, E = Montenegro,
    F = Rome, G = Mount Stromboli, H = Mount Etna, I = Malta

3. Any appropriate text. Pupils should draw on information from page 31 of the Study Book.
    E.g. Picture 1: Croatia used to have lots of hills and valleys near the coast. Picture 2: When sea levels rose,
    the valleys flooded and the hills became islands.

4. Italy — Croatia — Croatia — Italy — Italy

Extra Activities

- As a class, discuss why different countries are famous for different foods (e.g. different traditions, availability of certain ingredients), then ask pupils to name as many foods as they can think of that come from Italy. Briefly describe the history of pizza to pupils; pizza can be found in literature from over 2000 years ago — Virgil's *Aeneid* describes a savoury bread base covered with toppings as far back as 19 BC. However, it was in the late 18th century in Naples that it began to gain its popularity amongst the working classes as a quick, cheap snack food. As Italian immigrants moved to the USA, pizza grew even more in popularity, eventually reaching the global fame it has now. If possible, get pupils to create their own traditional, Roman-style pizzas (simple recipes can be found online).

- There are 450 different fish species living in the Adriatic Sea. Of these, 120 species are dangerously low in numbers due to overfishing. Search online for pictures of endangered fish of the Adriatic Sea, such as seahorses, Adriatic sturgeon and the ocean sunfish. Ask pupils to draw pictures of these fish and create group collages entitled 'Under the Adriatic Sea'.

- Ask pupils to plan a touring holiday of Italy, starting in the north and travelling south, finishing on a nearby island. Get pupils to use the internet and holiday brochures (if available) to help them decide where they would visit and what they would do there. Some possible locations to visit are: the Alps, Milan, Venice, Pisa, Florence, Mount Vesuvius, Pompeii, Rome, Sardinia and Sicily.

South-Eastern Europe

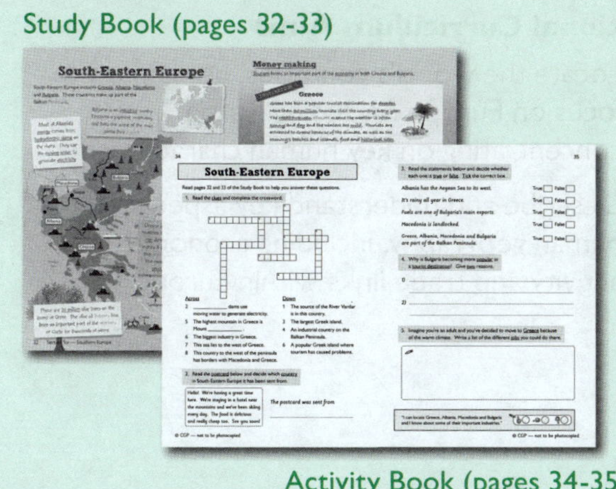

Study Book (pages 32-33)

Activity Book (pages 34-35)

National Curriculum Aims

- Locate the world's countries, using maps to focus on Europe, concentrating on key physical and human characteristics.

- Describe and understand key aspects of physical geography, including rivers, mountains and volcanoes.

- Describe and understand key aspects of human geography, including economic activity.

Introduction

This topic focuses on Greece, Albania, Macedonia and Bulgaria, which comprise part of the Balkan Peninsula. All or part of Bosnia and Herzegovina, Croatia, Kosovo, Montenegro, Romania, Serbia and Slovenia are often considered to make up the rest of this region.

Answers to Activity Book Questions

1. Across: 2 hydroelectric, 5 Olympus, 6 service, 7 Ionian, 8 Albania
   Down: 1 Macedonia, 3 Crete, 4 Bulgaria, 6 Santorini

2. *The postcard was sent from* Bulgaria.

3. False — False — True — True — True

4. E.g. It's cheaper than other similar tourist destinations, such as Greece. / There is snow in the mountains in winter which attracts tourists for winter sports like skiing.

5. Pupils should draw on information from the Study Book. E.g. shopkeeper, hotel owner, cleaner, receptionist, restaurant owner, chef, server, holiday resort worker, lifeguard, sheep/goat farmer.

Extra Activities

- Crete is known for its olive oil exportation and Greece is one of the top olive oil exporters in the world. Provide pupils with a blank map of Europe and ask them to look through the Study Book for examples of what goods other countries in Europe export (e.g. UK: cars and medicines, Germany: cars, chemicals, electronics and cheese, Netherlands: vegetables, Norway: oil and natural gas, Latvia: timber and wood products, Moldova: agricultural products and wine, Azerbaijan: oil, Bulgaria: electrical equipment, fuels and machinery). Ask pupils to design symbols to represent each export and mark the countries with the appropriate symbols. They should make a key to show what each symbol represents. Pupils could do their own research online about exports from European countries and add additional symbols to the map.

- Mount Olympus was notable in Greek mythology as the home of the twelve Greek gods known as the Olympians: Athena, Aphrodite, Artemis, Poseidon, Apollo, Demeter, Dionysus, Ares, Hermes, Hera, Hephaestus and Zeus. Split the class into small groups and give each group one god to research. They should find out the story that surrounds that god, what they were the god of, and who they were related to. Each group should then present their findings orally to the rest of the class.

- Tell pupils that the Ancient Greeks are known for inventing the theatre. Ancient Greek actors wore masks to show audiences what character they were playing and if they were happy or sad. Show pupils images of comedy and tragedy masks and ask them to create their own mask using paper. Alternatively, pupils could make their masks from papier mâché or sculpt them from modelling clay and paint them once dry.

Working Together

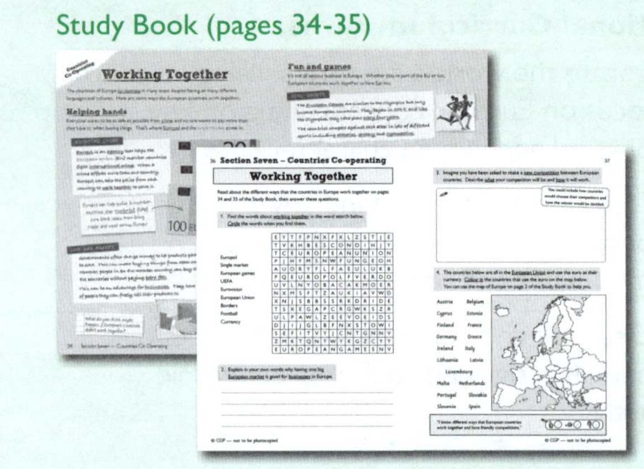

Study Book (pages 34-35)

Activity Book (pages 36-37)

National Curriculum Aims

- Locate the world's countries, using maps to focus on Europe (including Russia), concentrating on key human characteristics.

- Describe and understand key aspects of human geography, including economic activity and trade links within Europe.

Introduction

Co-operation and conflict between European countries has a long history, with countries forging (and breaking) strategic alliances. After the Second World War, there was a concerted effort to end conflicts. West European nations created the Council of Europe in 1949. A further treaty was signed between six nations (Belgium, France, Italy, Luxembourg, the Netherlands and West Germany) to have common management of steel and coal industries. Those six nations signed the Treaty of Rome in 1957, which created the European Economic Community. This community was gradually expanded, with the European Union being formally established in 1993.

Answers to Activity Book Questions

1. The locations of the words about Europe in the grid are here:

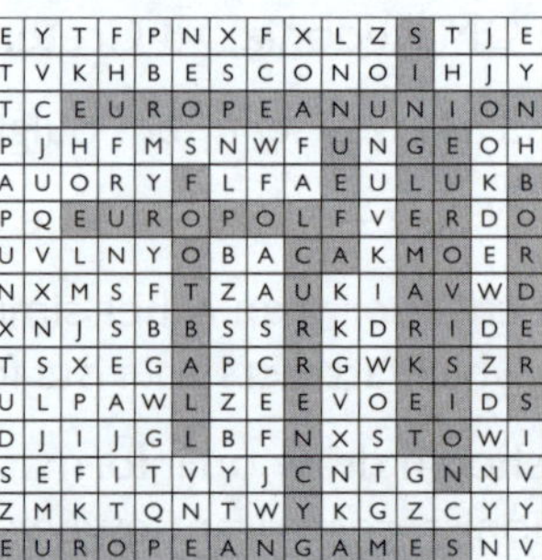

E	Y	T	F	P	N	X	F	X	L	Z	S	T	J	E
T	V	K	H	B	E	S	C	O	N	O	I	H	J	Y
T	C	E	U	R	O	P	E	A	N	U	N	I	O	N
P	J	H	F	M	S	N	W	F	U	N	G	E	O	H
A	U	O	R	Y	F	L	F	A	E	U	L	U	K	B
P	Q	E	U	R	O	P	O	L	F	V	E	R	D	O
U	V	L	N	Y	O	B	A	C	A	K	M	O	E	R
N	X	M	S	F	T	Z	A	U	K	I	A	V	W	D
X	N	J	S	B	B	S	S	R	K	D	R	I	D	E
T	S	X	E	G	A	P	C	R	G	W	K	S	Z	R
U	L	P	A	W	L	Z	E	E	V	O	E	I	D	S
D	J	I	J	G	L	B	F	N	X	S	T	O	W	I
S	E	F	I	T	V	Y	J	C	N	T	G	N	N	V
Z	M	K	T	Q	N	T	W	Y	K	G	Z	C	Y	Y
E	U	R	O	P	E	A	N	G	A	M	E	S	N	V

2. E.g. because it means that businesses have a large number of people to sell products to and they don't have to pay fees to move products between countries.

3. Any appropriate answer. E.g. A European baking competition. Each country holds their own competition. The winner from each country competes in a final, which is shown on television across Europe, and people phone in to vote for the winner.

4. The 19 countries listed should be correctly coloured in.

Extra Activities

- Divide the class into groups of about five pupils. Assign each group a European country to represent and have a football tournament, or a European games. Alternatively, pupils could be asked to vote on which sports (or other games) they want to have competitions for and plan a European-themed sports competition for the whole school, where different classes represent different countries.

- Divide the class into groups and ask them to solve a pretend crime. For example, the whole class could be told that there have been bank robberies in several countries and that the robber is hiding in a European city. Put 5 possible suspects and 5 possible locations up on the board. Give each group two clues, one about the appearance of the robber (e.g. he was wearing a hat) and one about their location (e.g. they are hiding on the Mediterranean coast). Each group's clues should be insufficient to solve the case by themselves. Every 5 minutes, let one pupil from each group visit another group and read their clues, then return to their own group to discuss it. The first group to solve the crime wins.

- Discuss with the class why certain countries might choose to not join the EU (or to leave it). For example, while being in the EU can make trade cheaper, it also costs money to be a member. Countries outside the EU can also control their own laws and regulations without having to adopt policies set by the EU.

GNT21